What Matters Most
20th Anniversary Edition

Featuring Ten Unreleased Interviews
Plus Special Guest Mayor Megan Barry

Conducted and Compiled by
Paul Samuel Dolman

South Beach

SOUTH BEACH PUBLISHING

Published by South Beach (USA)

404 Sweet Magnolia Court

Saint Augustine, Florida 32080

First printing, October 2017

Copyright © 2017 by Paul Samuel Dolman

All rights reserved. No part of this book may be reproduced, scanned, or distributed in any printed or electronic form without permission. Please do not participate in or encourage piracy of copyrighted materials in violation of the author's rights. Purchase only authorized editions.

LIBRARY OF CONGRESS CATALOGING-IN-PUBLICATION DATA

Paperback ISBN 978-1-890115-03-6

Printed in the United States of America

Cover Design ebook creation, and Paperback layout by
Matthew Wayne Selznick / MWS Media

While the author has made every effort to provide accurate telephone numbers, Internet addresses, and other contact information at the time of publication, neither the publisher nor the author assumes any responsibility for errors or for changes that occur after publication. Further, the publisher does not have any control over and does not assume any responsibility for author or third-party websites or their content

For my father
Who, through his life
Has shown me
What matters most

Foreword

Way back in 1997 I started asking people around Nashville and Tennessee, what matters most. Twenty years later I'm still inquiring, only now my quest has expanded to a more global walkabout via my podcast and extensive travels.

In honor of the original publication, here are ten of my favorite interviews from the original, plus ten more that have never been released, and a brand new conversation with the current Mayor of Nashville, Megan Barry.

I have also included a snippet from each of the original participants as well as a brief commentary highlighting something about them or the nature of us coming together.

We live in a time of infinite information and yet wisdom appears hard to come by. I felt these dialogues were loaded with practical and esoteric truths that when embodied, could transform the quality of one's life.

Good truth is timeless.

What does matter most?

Let's turn the page and see...

SUCCESS

To laugh often and much; to win the respect of intelligent people and the affection of children; to earn the appreciation of honest critics and endure the betrayal of false friends; to appreciate beauty, to find the best in others; to leave the world a bit better, whether by a healthy child, a garden patch or a redeemed social condition; to know even one life has breathed easier because you have lived. This is to have succeeded.

-Ralph Waldo Emerson

INTRODUCTION

My life and this book are about the same thing: building bridges between people for the greater good. In writing *What Matters Most*, my goal was to take the wonderfully diverse, collective wisdom of Nashville and raise it up to a place of unification, and in the process show that, despite our superficial differences, despite how we may define success, or what name we might call God, deep down in our core we are all basically the same. Dr. T.B. Boyd said it quite well, "We may have come over on different ships, but we are all in the same boat."

In our culture, success is mostly defined in terms of money and status. The goal of this book is to broaden the paradigm of success.

It is about the qualities people possess — how they see and react to life — and how that contributes to their success.

The book reflects intimate interviews I conducted with 40 noteworthy Nashvillians. Each person answered my questions, sharing wisdom in his or her own words.

These people are examples of what can happen when we get in touch with our hearts, follow our hearts, and truly live life. There is potential within each of us to do the same and make a difference in the world.

This book is also about tolerance and acceptance. I ask that you read it with an open heart. I hope you can see through the theoretical divergence to a common ground where ideas intersect — like making a contribution to your fellow man and selflessly serving the greater whole.

Throughout the interviews, I found myself repeatedly inspired by the participants. While I did not always agree with their opinions, I greatly respected their convictions and their choice to share them so openly and honestly.

I encourage you to focus on the transcendent qualities of the human spirit, rather than how these people might be different from you.

This book is a way of saying, "look how different we are ... but how much alike."

For me, success is really about the dignity of the human spirit and one's ability to reach out to others and make a positive difference in the world. No act of love, kindness or compassion is ever too small. I want to thank you for choosing my book, and invite you to join me, and my guests on a wonderful journey of discovery as we talk about and share *What Matters Most*.

Paul Samuel Dolman

Nashville, TN January 1997

What Matters Most
20th Anniversary Edition

Mayor Megan Barry
(New 20th Anniversary Content)

"What matters most to me is making sure that whatever I'm doing, whatever imprint I create, I leave somebody feeling better because they've had that interaction with me."

Megan Barry is the seventh mayor of the Metropolitan Government of Nashville and Davidson County. She was elected on September 10, 2015.

Backstory: Megan and I met almost twenty years ago and she has been (a) both a fabulous friend and someone who, by the way she lives, inspires you to take your own life to a higher place. When the decision was made to release a 20-year anniversary edition of What Matters Most, I immediately knew that I wanted her to be my special guest.

PSD: I've been waiting for years to say the words Mayor Megan Barry. Do you remember conversations back at Fido's while having lunch? We batting ideas around and you said, "Maybe I'll run City Council.

MB: I do and you said, "The sky's the limit."

PSD: So the million-dollar question is why is the whole world moving to Nashville?

MB: Nashville is an amazing place at the moment. I think it's a combination of being progressive but also pro-business. But I believe it's really about the people and let me tell you where I see the differences. People in Nashville say what can I do for you, not what can you do for me. This really just shows. I think that's why people want to come here. They can feel that sense of community almost instantly.

PSD: When I moved there from the Northeast after college, people were so nice I was literally suspicious. Afterward I'd be embarrassed when they proved to be sincere.

MB: They are absolutely sincere when they say what can I do for you. I think it's very real.

PSD: When did you first come to town?

MB: I first came to town in 1991 to attend Vanderbilt

and get my MBA. My intent was to stay 18 months because I, too, was not a southerner. In fact I was coming from London when I moved here. My goal was to get here, get in, get out and be gone. Funny, now I can't imagine living any other place in the whole world.

PSD: I wish I had a dollar for everyone who came for a few months or years and stayed for 20 or more.

MB: Yes, I completely agree with you. I do believe that when people get here they just take a look around and say, 'This is not only a beautiful place, but a place that's really easy and kind.' I think we're really a kind place.

PSD: Megan, what inspired you to get so deeply involved on a civic level?

MB: I think that for me being inspired every day is this idea that this is really all about people. I get the chance to sit in this seat at this moment. In fact I have a quote on my desk that says, 'Power is about waking up every day and making a difference in somebody else's life.' I get to sit in this seat in this minute and that gives me the chance. I also have a staff of people who work hard every day on all of the very complex issues that we need to address when we think about Nashville being a growing place. So this opportunity also comes with challenges in transportation, affordable housing, education, equity, and job access.

PSD: There's no feeling like positively touching and changing a life.

MB: Yes, absolutely. I mean, one of the initiatives that we are rolling out this summer, which I'm so excited about, is a youth violence summit. When I came into office we went out and actually asked the youth in our community, what do you need from the adults in your life? One kid, who was spot on, said, 'You adults ask us to walk a tightrope but we need a safety net. We need a place that when we fall something's going to catch us and we need hope.'

So what we did is we challenged the community this year to come up with hope and opportunities. We called it Opportunity Now. We have ten thousand jobs for kids aged 14 to 24 in paid meaningful experiences that we are connecting our youth to the summer. By the way, some folks in the community said, 'Why don't we just start with like 500 jobs and see how it goes? I said absolutely not! Ten thousand is our goal and we've had close to eight thousand kids who've gone into the portal to be connected to those jobs.

So that starts a great cycle of helping people first lift themselves out of poverty, and it also gives them something to do.

PSD: There's nothing like purpose and each one of those children will touch five people who live in proximity to them. So it's really 50,000 maybe 100,000 lives you touch.

Do you feel any added pressure being the first female Mayor of Nashville?

MB: It's not so much the pressure, but one of the things I think is funny is that I'm not the face that people expect. So recently I was at a groundbreaking for a new venture that we have here and I was talking to the CEO and the CFO, both who were male, and one of their staff members came over and said, 'Oh, we've got to get started. The mayor's here, you know.' Then they said, 'That's exciting. Where is he?

(Laughs) I turned to them and said, 'You've been

talking to her for the last 10 minutes.' They looked utterly shocked and asked, 'Wait, you're the mayor?

PSD: I love that.

MB: You could just see both of their faces like, gosh, you're really not what we were expecting.

PSD: In a bit of irony, their advance people are now in the 10,000 jobs pool looking for new summer work.

MB: (Laughs) I'm sure they are. Anyway, it was pretty funny.

PSD: You mentioned challenges. What are the biggest challenges right now for this great city? Everybody is talking about the traffic. That's an obvious one. I heard you address light rail and some other progressive ideas in a speech. Of course, having a light rail system would not be considered progressive in Europe; in fact it is standard.

MB: The idea of progressive has different connotations depending on where you are. Our challenges continue to be about how do you maintain and stabilize communities that are seeing tremendous growth? How do you make sure that the existing residents benefit from, but are not impacted by or displaced by, the growth that is coming? Because change is inevitable and how do we make sure that everybody in Davidson County is feeling that prosperity.

Are they feeling that prosperity and access to opportunities and job training, housing, education and quality of life?

PSD: We joked about it in the beginning, but the rate of growth has shocked me. It's been a bit of a runaway train. I mean, you're all riding the bull. No one expected this sort of mega growth that fast.

MB: I think you're right. If you look comprehensively at the role of cities and how important cities have become to our overall U.S. economy, the growth of cities is absolutely on the rise. Nashville just happens to be lucky and at the forefront of some of that. People want to live in urban centers. They are young folks or want to be in close proximity to places where they live and where they work and where they play. Nashville has definitely been the beneficiary of that.

PSD: On the personal side, what's the biggest challenge you have found doing the job? You've named all these very complex things and you have a crack staff, but it all falls on your desk here. You're not one who passes the buck.

MB: Well, I tell you, I think you just hit it. It's balancing all those different priorities because you do have limited capital and you have limited human resources. But we have unlimited potential. So how do you harness that energy that is the government? But also remember that government cannot solve all the problems. So one of the things that we've been very focused on has been to develop what we call private public partnerships. You see how I put the private first? We absolutely have to rely on the private sector, the not- for-profit sector, and the faith community to help us move the needle on some of these complex problems. We have to collectively come up with creative solutions.

PSD: I'm thinking of my dear friend John Ingram and the great work he's been able to do by creating the Entrepreneur Center downtown. That organization has done amazing things all over the community.

MB: John is fantastic and so is the center. So it's getting other people involved beyond just writing checks or making new laws.

PSD: How do you find the personal balance? Do you still get out to Radnor Lake and take a walk? You're laughing because it must sound like a ludicrous question.

MB: I'm laughing because yesterday I found myself on a Sunday afternoon with the wonderful opportunity to walk to the Belcourt Theater and see a movie, which I don't get to do very often. To just sit and eat some popcorn and then walk, which was delightful. I try to do that. I try to find those moments so I do get out and walk. I also do hot yoga. Hot yoga is my solace. To just be in a room where you're focused for one hour, on your body and breathing. Moving helps me stay energized for any of the things that come.

PSD: Plus there are no phones in yoga, right?

MB: That's right.

PSD: Do you meditate? Have you incorporated that as a tool in your process to be peaceful?

MB: The time during yoga is my opportunity to just quiet the mind and focus on my breath. To consciously move your body in ways that are very spiritual.

PSD: You just mentioned the word time and recently you posted that the once little Max, your son, is graduating college. I remember the big news when you were pregnant. So I staggered away from that news amazed at how quickly time can pass.

MB: I know. Isn't that crazy? How did that happen? Twenty-two years just like that, my gosh.

In terms of time, people are always very curious about the first hundred days that you are in office. They would often say, 'In those 100 days, what have you done?' Well, on my phone I have a counter that counts backwards so I know that today I have eight hundred and one days before my re-election. I know that I'm guaranteed those 801 days to make a difference. I mean, we're guaranteed no days but you get my point. This idea that we have a timeline and it's ticking backwards. Because like you mentioned, we all know how really fast it passes.

PSD: I just interviewed a former Nashville icon, Joel Solomon.

MB: I love Joe. He's awesome and I know him well.

Paul: He's great. He had a death sentence when he was diagnosed with a terminal kidney disease. He ended up beating it, but he said that getting a death sentence was the best thing that ever happened to him because it created an urgency and a preciousness to his life.

MB: That's so true. Like I said, every morning I look at my phone and think, OK that's how much time I have. So what are we going to get done today?

PSD: You could plug that in same perspective into the bigger picture. Shifting gears, Nashville is a great beacon of progressive policies and thinking, but why is the South generally so politically and culturally regressive?

MB: Well, we have a history in the South that has not necessarily always brought everybody with us. I do think you're seeing incremental movement like Mayor Mitch Landrieu down in New Orleans taking down statues that are symbolic of a different time.

PSD: There was a lot of controversy and resistance around that.

MB: But you know, to Mitch's credit, he said, 'Look, this is our past but not what we want for our future.' I think that is where cities like Nashville, Louisville and places like that are moving. We are getting much better about saying yes, we have to recognize our past and you can't forget it. In fact we just put up one of the first monuments to the civil rights movement in Nashville, which was a huge center for the movement. But we haven't really celebrated that as much as we need to. So we are recognizing our history but also realizing that our future is what we have to be focused on.

PSD: You're referring to the lunch counter sit-ins that took place here.

MB: Yes, they sure did. And the nonviolence movement came out of Nashville. I think that, if you look at the legacy of Nashville, this is not a place that that erupts in violence because we do have this process.

I like to think of it this way because this is my management style. I think you try to take conflict and turn it into conversation. But then you have to take that conversation and turn it into action because you can talk until everybody is blue in the face. But if you actually never move past the conversation to action then that just leads to frustration. And Nashville really has a history of being more inclusive than other cities throughout the south. There's a long history here of openness and being inclusive.

PSD: It's a tribute that shows the foresight of the leaders we had in the past.

MB: They were great and I do. You know, it's interesting you should say that because what we've seen over the last probably two years is that a lot of our great voices have died. I think now is a time where we need that younger demographic, that younger generation to step up and fill the shoes of folks who have come before, like the folks that you're mentioning.

PSD: Men like my mentor Nelson Andrews, who always spoke very highly of you.

MB: Thank you for passing that on. I always had immense respect for Nelson and a great fondness because he was really an incredible civic and community leader.

PSD: On the national scene, as a woman and also a mayor in a big city, what are your feelings around the rise of Trump and the kind of things he has incited or encouraged?

MB: I always worry that any time you've got extremes, they will manifest themselves in how people talk with each other and deal with each other. Clearly there's fear in communities that are concerned about what the potential national stage can do to those communities, especially those communities that are much more fragile.

I'm concerned about it as well, from our folks who are undocumented, to folks who rely on the federal government for programs like Head Start and housing. Those are all things that, as we look at a budget that gets proposed, you can see where somebody's priorities are based on their budget.

PSD: Yet in the end aren't we only as good as what we do for the least amongst us?

MB: I concur, yes.

PSD: What would you tell young women who listen to you today about what's possible for someone who has dreams?

MB: I would say, if you see a door walk through it. You never know what's going to be on the other side of that door and you never know where the next door will lead. I have an undergraduate degree in elementary education. I spent about five minutes in the classroom before I figured out that that really is the hardest job in the whole world. I've got an MBA from Vanderbilt, so two very different loves.

But by combining the two in this job, it's a really nice way to be somebody who cares deeply and wants to see people succeed from that educator perspective, but also has that pragmatic business side to run a complex organization that is the city of Nashville. Now I never would have put those two pieces together and said, 'Oh, (that) my next progression is being the mayor. I had conversations with people like you at a coffee house and as we talked, those doors opened and I walked through them.

Then the other part, of course, is after you walk through that door, take your hand and reach back and pull the next person through that door with you because that's our obligation for all of us. We have to reach back.

PSD: Where did this beautiful sense of optimism come from? Were you always like this?

Meg: I don't know. I think I've always been this way. I believe if you love people and you want people to be successful that you have an optimism that that just comes with that. Also, so much of this is mirrored in my Catholic faith and my Catholic upbringing, which is that idea that you serve and that you do that by remembering the people who are the least among us. That you make sure, as Pope Francis recently said during Lent, 'we give up our lattes and our glasses of wine. But what we really need to do is give up our indifference to people who are struggling. The ones who are un-housed, who are poor, who are jobless, who are incarcerated. We give up our indifference.'

I think that's where my sense of service comes from.

PSD: What I love about your spirituality is that your feet are on the ground and hands are giving out the fishes and loaves. It's not just an esoteric paradigm.

MB: Absolutely. We actually have to do something to get that conversation to action.

PSD: I was once having a conversation over lunch with your husband and he said, 'You sound just like my wife. You two need to get together. I think you guys will become great friends.' He introduced us and his prediction was correct.

MB: I love that. I have him to thank as well for many, many things.

PSD: Before we let you get back to really important things, what matters most to you, Megan?

MB: What matters most to me is making sure that whatever I'm doing, whatever imprint I create, I leave somebody feeling better because they've had that interaction with me.

PSD: So it's a one-to-one experience. It's not this big thing; it's just what's in front of you.

MB: The big things matter, but eventually everything

is actually about people. So what matters most is that after you and I have had this conversation, you feel better for it. That I left you with a feeling of hope and optimism and connectivity and that you will then go on and have that next conversation with somebody and spread the same thing.

PSD: Well then, you were radically successful, because that's how I feel every time I've had the privilege to sit with you. I remember saying, 'I hope you run for mayor.'

MB: Thank you for putting that out to the universe, Paul. I so appreciate it and our time together today. I feel like we've done something that matters.

Bill Moyers

"Never get too old or grow too sophisticated to stop being a student. I don't know of any better way to cope with the perils of life, the hazards of existence, and the demands of society, than to learn something new every day."

Journalist, Author, and Educator

Backstory: I have admired Bill Moyers for as long as I can remember. Perhaps it started when I was driving across the country in a beat up, old two-seat Datsun in search of answers and came across a tattered copy of his book, A World of Ideas, in a tiny bookstore somewhere out in the middle of Arizona. Or maybe it was when I was feeling lost in Los Angeles while wondering if there was any meaning in life. There was Bill talking to Joseph Campbell about the Power of Myth and how it could play a role in shaping our lives.

Bill Moyers work has changed my life in so many positive ways.

So when I read that one of the participants in the original What Matters Most, John Seigenthaler, was hosting an event in Nashville for Mr. Moyers, I had the ambitious idea of including this icon in my book as a special guest.

Through some good old-fashioned detective work, I found out Bill would first be a guest on John's television show, A Word on Words. Long story short- I snuck into the studio and with Mr. Seigenthaler's blessing and Bill's generosity, I got the interview you will read below.

As an extra bonus that evening, Wynonna Judd sat next to me in the audience. After Bill's presentation concluded, she and I ended up sharing an epic two-hour soul conversation. As we shared a hug goodbye, Wynonna declared, "Hey, I want to be in this book too."

I said 'yes' and she turned out to be interview number forty, which concluded the work.

PSD: Do you feel your series of interviews with Joseph

Campbell for the *Power Of Myth* series was a professional or personal turning point?

BM: I don't see it as a turning point because I find a certain consistency to my curiosity over the years, of which the Campbell series was certainly one manifestation. It was probably the most popular series I ever did in terms of the response. I didn't anticipate its success. The series aired with almost no promotion and no publicity to a very small rating by commercial standards and modest by public television standards.

But word of mouth spread, almost contagiously. People were calling up public television stations and pleading with them to repeat the series. It just grew into a phenomenon in its own right that I never anticipated, didn't intend, and didn't know how to evaluate.

PSD: You started out in traditional media, yet your journalistic path has taken on a very spiritual element over the years. Was there a catalyst earlier in your life or career that shifted your paradigm? Or were you always curious, with this road just a natural extension of your quest?

BM: Well, I am a journalist first and foremost. I started studying journalism at the age of sixteen, and have had some detours along the way. I went into government politics for seven years. I studied theology and ethics for four-and-a-half years. So I was aware of the importance of religion in people's lives, unlike journalists who have not had any theological training.

I knew that, for millions of Americans, faith matters. Faith is a subjective reality that drives, animates, and influences behavior. It was natural for me, when I had the chance, to try to cover that beat as a journalist.

Because I knew it was important, and I had already covered everything else: government, politics, economics, and sports. Sometimes even the weather.

So I don't think there was any one thing or catalyst. It's not that I am on any kind of mission. I just recognize the role that religion plays in millions of people's lives, and any time I cover it, the response confirms that intuition. I do a lot of conventional journalism: documentaries on public education, documentaries on politics and government in Washington, the environment. But nothing I do has the impact like the programs I do that deal with religion in one way or another.

PSD: Do you have a personal definition of success?

BM: I never have thought about that. (He pauses) It's being able to have an idea for something original and see it emerge as a television series six months or two years later. It's the knowledge that, as a public educator, I have one of the largest classrooms in the country. Television is a university without walls. Life is a continuing course of adult education and I have a great classroom, into which I invite some of the most interesting people, stories, and ideas of our time.

So success for me is knowing that I have had an idea that I can share with a larger audience whose own world is then enlarged by that experience.

PSD: Does the arc of this process bring you a deep sense of joy?

BM: Yes, though my greatest pleasure is spending time with my family —my wife, children, and my grandkids. But it certainly gives me the greatest professional satisfaction.

PSD: If your grandchildren asked you for a little guidance, as they were about to go out in the world on life's path, what would you tell them?

BM: Never get too old or grow too sophisticated to stop being a student. I don't know of any better way to cope with the perils of life, the hazards of existence, and the demands of society, than to learn something new every day. If people consider themselves lifelong students, no matter what they do, they are never going to get bored. They may have periods of doubt, they may be out of a job, they may be sick or have infirmity, or lose friends and family. But as long as you think of every day as an invitation to learn, you will never find a day that fails you.

PSD: What do you do to stay grounded and get in touch with your inner self?

BM: I do just what I advise other people to do. I am always listening, reading, and enjoying the company of people who know more than I do. I don't come away from a lunch with strangers or with friends where I haven't learned or shared something. So keep good company — people who can teach you something.

PSD: Do you ever think about how you might like to be remembered?

BM: I really don't. I haven't ever been asked that question! For one thing, I don't think people in television are remembered very long. It is an ephemeral, passing, fleeting, transient medium. The best a journalist can do is serve his time and move on. So I don't really think of being remembered, except by my family. I want them to remember me for the fun we had together and the intimacy we shared.

PSD: After all these years, what keeps you going?

BM: People like you who think it matters.

Sir John Templeton
(New 20th Anniversary Content)

As a pioneer in both financial investment and philanthropy, the late Sir John Templeton spent a lifetime encouraging open-mindedness. If he had not sought new paths, he once said, "I would have been unable to attain so many goals." The motto that Sir John created for his foundation, "How little we know, how eager to learn," exemplified his philosophy both in the financial markets and in his groundbreaking methods of philanthropy.

Backstory: I had heard about John Templeton for years and even had a dream where we met. A few years after my original version of What Matters Most was released, I sent a letter inquiring if I could come to the Bahamas and interview him. To my surprise his assistant called and asked me if April 9th would work? I laughed and said, "How crazy, that's my birthday!"

Everything worked out well with Sir John, 'please just call me John,' being very open and warm. I stayed with him for a couple of hours and we covered a lot of subjects. He had as many questions for me as I had for him. He loaded me up with books and invited me to come back and stay in touch.

I kept my promise on all fronts and he was generous with his guidance and wisdom. A couple years later I brought the author, Neale Donald Walshe, who wrote Conversations With God, down to Nassau to meet John. The hope was that they could work together to bring more people to spirituality.

Sir John was such a humble man and I did feel a sense of loss when I heard of his passing. He stays on with me in my own curiosity and pursuit of the divine mysteries.

PSD: Growing up in Winchester, Tennessee, did you feel you were a spiritual person?

SJT: Well I was active in the Cumberland Presbyterian Church and I always thought from the time I was able to think that God didn't create humanity without a purpose. God created humanity to be helpful in God's ongoing purposes so that it's up to each of us with what talent God has given us to try to be helpful.

PSD: When you were young, what was your primary method of connecting with the source?

SJT: Reading mainly. I read more than other children with the idea of learning the basic realities of learning the reasons why God created humanity, what purpose God might have had for creating me. So it came quite naturally I must say there was nothing dramatic. I was always interested though, I was always fascinated and so I did a very large amount of reading.

PSD: Why do you think God created you personally?

SJT: Honestly, it's a tremendous mystery. I think it's a very worshipful mystery as to why anybody is created. But the closest answer that any writer has come at so far is that God created all these billions of humans, each one different but each one with certain talents, to use those talents to accelerate God's creativity. God has been creating the visible universe for 15 billion years but it's only in the last 4,000 years that humans have learned to read and write, that humans have really been able to take an active part in speeding up the rate of creativity, and it's really astounding and very impressive that almost every week some human being comes up with some new concept or new invention that really accelerates creativity. And quite likely that's what God had in mind when he or she designed us.

PSD: So John Templeton is part of the creativity?

SJT: I try to be but there are 4 billion other people trying too. So I'm not outstanding but I do try to be helpful. I try to do things that would be helpful, that would make the world a better place.

PSD: Was the Templeton Foundation and the Templeton Prizes created with that primary intention?

SJT: Yes. In my career I felt that the talents God had given me were to help investors make less stupid mistakes in their investments. So my lone career in Wall Street was to help people make less stupid mistakes. (Laughs) But all that time I thought perhaps there are other things that I can do that would be more helpful. So the first program I started was 27 years ago while thinking about Alfred Nobel who had set up The Nobel Prize for programs in physics, programs in chemistry, programs in medicine and so forth. But he seemed to have overlooked the most important one, which is a program in more spiritual information.

Nobel had to give five prizes and the prizes at the time were 70,000 British pounds. So I decided to give a prize of 75,000 British pounds in order to say to the world that programs in spiritual information were more important than physics or chemistry. So we did that. But Nobel's estate has been very well managed so that now he gives prizes of 650,000 British pounds and so the Templeton prize has been increased to 700,000, almost 10 times what we started with so we can always give a larger reward for spiritual progress and progress in medicine.

PSD: How has it worked?

SJD: It's been reasonably successful. We never choose who is to win. We invite famous people to be the judges. Each judge serves three years, there are 9 judges and they usually come from five different religions and they decide who has done something truly beneficial, truly original in any religion and I rejoice that all 29 winners have been totally different, no two alike and all of them have done something wonderful and new. So it's working out well but so far it has not been as influential as we had hoped it to be. It has not reached as many minds in the world as the Nobel prizes have.

So we're always trying to find experts who can help us to reach more people. For example this year, next month, for the first time we're having the awards ceremony in a Communist nation. We're having it in Moscow in the Kremlin in the private chapel of the patriarch of the Russian Orthodox Church. We think it will be newsworthy that now, even in the great Communist center, they are studying religion. So we believe this will reach more minds than any of our previous years.

PSD: Why do you think spirituality, which may be the most important topic on Earth, is so relegated to the 'back of the bus'?

SJT: Well, that's a big question and the answers are uncertain and highly complex.

PSD: Of course there's not a sound bite for something like that, but what's your take?

SJT: To try to help your story here, if I had to put the answer in one word, it's 'human egotism'. All throughout all religions, not just our own Christianity, but throughout all religions, each one has tended to say 'we've got the total proof'. Now if you do think you've got the total proof and you meet somebody who has a different idea, it's your duty to convert them, or else kill them. Sadly, that has happened throughout time. All religions, not just Christianity, but all religions have killed other people because the person doing the killing thought he had the total proof. But that's not religion, that's human egotism. It's incredibly egotistic for any human to think he knows the totality of God. But it is that egotism that has caused the so-called religious wars. In my opinion there has never been a war about religion, it's a war about human egotism.

So we're trying to change that mindset. It's a mindset to think you're so smart that you know it all. So we're trying to make people humble. We're trying to make them think, gee, how little I know. God is 100 or 1000 times greater than I understand so when you meet somebody who has a different idea you don't try to convert him. You say, gee, thank you for coming to me. Help me, maybe I can learn more from you. Then everybody loves each other and you can't have wars if you're all trying to learn from each other.

PSD: You wrote a wonderful book about that which I've read, *The Humble Approach*. In it you made an interesting point: that while science is ever-evolving, theology or religious dogma is stuck with doctrine that's 2,000 years old or even 5,000 years old. This is from a time when people thought the world was flat and unfortunately the dogma is locked in a place where it says you can't even question it, that this is the final truth. Is this what the Templeton Foundation is trying to open up?

SJT: Yes that's right, to change the mindset so that people will be enthusiastic rather than resistant to new concepts.

PSD: As you look towards the heavens on a clear evening, what do you feel when you realize there are over 100 billion stars in the Milky Way Galaxy, and perhaps infinite galaxies in the physical universe?

SJT: Very humble of course but also far more worshipful. Before I knew those scientific or those astronomic facts, I tended to worship God as if he were a sort of a kind old king above. I worshiped him but I find it far easier and I feel more enthusiastic about worshiping a God who is the God of all including the mysterious intelligence on 100's of billions of other planets.

PSD: How does a person cultivate humility?

SJT: I don't have the answer to that. I would like to see what you write about it. It makes me more and more humble to hear about communications, which is your field. The total quality of information is now doubling about every three years, some people say faster. But if information is doubling every three years that means in 30 years the world will have 1,000 times as much information as now, and in 60 years a million times as much information as we have now. That makes me very humble. Also it makes me concerned that won't it be sad 60 years from now if we can say we don't have any more spiritual information. We have a million times more information but not much more spiritual information. That would be tragic.

PSD: Also, what especially strikes me in this age of abundant information, is that there seems to be an absence of wisdom. When you talk about spiritual information to me I translate that into wisdom. How do we weed out the facts and figures and find our truth?

SJT: I don't know but that's a great question and maybe you can find people who will help you with that. When my children were young I refused to buy a television because I thought it would do more harm than good.

So now I think it might be helpful if television sets would only receive beneficial programs. There are some beneficial programs on the air, but in my opinion far too few. People could make receiving sets that would receive only the beneficial ones and then their families and their children would get beneficial information.

PSD: What was your philosophy as a parent?

SJT: The same as any other parent. God obviously decided that his children, humanity would not live forever. That humanity would grow and progress through having children and grandchildren. Instead of trying to make a body that never deteriorates, make it easy to reproduce. So producing children is a sacred duty. I think that most people tend to make their children dependent, in other words, because they love their children they want to help their children but they help them so greatly that the child becomes dependent rather than self-reliant. So I tried not to be too controlling, not to be too influential, let them develop personally. My family, my parents did that too. It was not unusual in Franklin County in the old days. I can't ever remember my father or my mother telling me to do something or not do something because they thought it would make me childish, they wanted me to grow up and learn for myself what to do and what not to do. And I think that's what parents should pay more attention to now, trying to transform each of their children into an adult rather than keeping them a child.

PSD: Do you believe, at some point, through science,

we can discover God?

SJT: Yes, though that's not precisely the right way to put it. If you do a lot of thinking about it you come to the conclusion that almost all the sciences help in discovering God. You've illustrated one already with the number of stars in our galaxy and the unfathomable number of galaxies. That surely teaches you about God. It doesn't take the place of the ancient scriptures but it enlarges your concept above what the people could possibly imagine when the scriptures were written. So in effect astronomy is a method of theology and so is medicine. Medicine is teaching you about your internal nature and particularly your mental nature and so forth, all of which is helping you to understand God better. So sciences are not in conflict, at least most sciences are not in conflict with theology, they are methods of theology.

PSD: What advice would you give a young person heading out into the world?

SJT: To be humble, of course, would be one thing. Another would be to have a purpose in your life. Don't live your life aimlessly. Don't live your life for your personal pleasure. Live your life for some purpose. And lastly of the big matters is to try to have unlimited love for every human being with never any exception. That goes a long way. If you can really gradually train yourself to feel unlimited love for every person on earth, never an exception, then all the other things fall in line.

PSD: And you can cultivate that, can't you?

SJT: Yes. It's not easy, but it can be done.

PSD: What solutions would you offer for the problems going on in the world these days?

SJT: I would emphasis free and fair competition. The civilizations that have restricted free competition have suffered. In many ways they suffer by egotism, they suffer by wars, and they suffer by suppressing progress and so forth. But those civilizations who have welcomed free competition have made amazingly rapid improvements. If you take an index of the nations who have the greatest amount of free competition, they turn out to be the wealthiest nations. These things are studied carefully by the Freedom Foundation and others and published yearly. You take a list of the nations who have the greatest freedom and the nations that have the greatest prosperity, and they're almost in line with each other. If you want your nation to be prosperous, if you want your nation to be peaceful and happy, have maximum free competition.

PSD: Are you worried at all in terms of the growth going the other way and threatening the environment through pollution, waste, and overpopulation?

SJT: Well, there are always problems and that is an important one. It's obvious and there's never been a period in human history when they didn't have problems. Problems tend to be overcome by this free competition we're talking about. Nations that take too much time to wage war don't prosper or don't progress. Nations that don't improve the environment by better seeds, better methods of agriculture and so forth, tend to be static or even regressive, whereas those that are open-minded, those that are always looking for new ideas, they tend to progress. So free and fair competition in the long run overcomes most of those problems.

PSD: What would you advise someone who is dealing

with great adversity in their life?

SJT: Prayer is marvelously beneficial and so is meditation. But in addition to that, you want to have a positive outlook, in other words, almost everything that happens to you is in some way an opportunity. When I discovered that I had to pay my own way through college, I thought it was a tragedy and yet it still was an opportunity. Now I was going out and not only trying to get good grades in order to get scholarships, I learned to work hard. I learned to do more than one thing at a time and do two or three things at a time. So I wound up at the end of my three years the top scholar at Yale, which I wouldn't have done otherwise. So if you think about each of your problems in life, you can also find that there is in some aspects an opportunity.

PSD: I have to bring this up. During your tenure at Yale, didn't you help pay for some of your school costs with your winnings from poker?

SJT: Yes. (Laughs) Because when you're faced with a necessity... I noticed that Yale had a lot of wealthy boys and they played poker and they played poker just for the fun of it but I was sitting at games not for the fun of it, I would calculate out the arithmetic, so I usually came out ahead.

PSD: When you were young, were you out to make your first million?

SJT: Well, yes. But more than that, in order to make the first million, I felt I had to be useful. I couldn't make the million by just wanting to. I had to go out and give people something. But another aspect to it that you haven't mentioned yet is that, in all of my lifetime of experience with wealthy people, they're not any happier than poor people.

PSD: Yes, it's an old cliché that money doesn't bring happiness. So you have found it to be true?

SJT: Yes.

PSD: What has brought you the most happiness in your life?

SJT: The feeling of being useful. I'm happier right now than I've ever been.

PSD: That's beautiful.

SJT: Because some of these programs that our foundations are helping to pay for are beginning to have very beneficial results.

PSD: My theory is there's no difference in being useful in the big picture or useful in the little picture. If it's holding your grandson in the ocean or giving away 700,000 pounds.

SJT: Yes. The big picture really consists of a lot of little pictures. One picture for example is one of our foundations made a survey as recently as six years ago and we could find only three graduate schools of medicine that were giving any course in spirituality as a method of health. These were sort of small medical schools run by the very strict religions. But we decided that spirituality certainly was a benefit to health and that it ought to be taught in medical school. So we tried to be helpful by...if they would start a course in spirituality as the method of healing, as a supplement. Spirituality is a supplement to medical healing. And now, only six years later, we have subsidized 19 such courses and there have been 41 other graduate schools of medicine who have started six courses without our subsidy, so that now almost

50% of all medical schools in North America offer courses in spirituality to supplement medicine. Only six years! That gives me great joy.

PSD: You're planting seeds, aren't you? Do you think it's ego that would deny a connection between spirit, mind and body?

SJT: It never occurred to me it was ego, but I think most people think it is. That's an excellent observation.

PSD: How can the average Joe—someone reading this who's got two kids and a mortgage to pay—be useful?

SJT: Examine your talents. For example, I examined my talents and I had absolutely zero talents in music. But you've examined your talents and you have talents in music and in communication. Find your gift and follow that path.

PSD: When you commune with your inner source, do you feel you are in touch with a very definitive guidance? One some might call that still, small voice?

SJT: It's definitive but not small. Though with practice it can be cultivated.

PSD: God is so infinite the language is not up to the task. Even in our minds, even if the thoughts about it are infinitely inadequate.

SJT: That's right and to me that makes God much more worshipful. When I was a child I thought in terms of the way God is described in the Old Testament and I worshiped him. But I find much more enthusiasm worshiping a God who is a million times bigger than that.

PSD: I cant' even comprehend infinity.

SJT: The fact that I can't comprehend it makes it worshipful and expansive.

PSD: Do you find the universe or God to be a loving Presence rather than the Old Testament manifestation of a vengeful sort of deity that if we don't do just the right thing on a very narrow path, boy, are we going to get it.

SJT: I do.

PSD: Since they always come no matter what how high up on the human totem pole one climbs, what is the greatest challenge facing you today?

SJT: Time. You can put it in different ways but one thing I suppose is, I only have a few years left and I want to make each year count. Other than that, it's to encourage those many entrepreneurs who are trying various ways to multiply spiritual information, especially through scientific research to supplement all the wonderful ancient scriptures. So I look for ways to encourage those people and there are lots of them, more and more all the time, by donations or by books or anything else. Encourage them to work harder to multiply spiritual information. I'm really hopeful that in a short time—a short time is two centuries—humans can understand 100 times as much of our God as we have understood before and that would be tremendously beneficial.

PSD: A noble quest, but not an easy one.

It's not easy and it starts out slowly, like say, in medicine. For example, my grandfather in Franklin County, Tennessee was a medical doctor. But he had never heard of a germ and he couldn't conceive that Alexander Fleming was going to invent penicillin to kill germs and he didn't know germs existed, you see.

But because medical people always encouraged them and rewarded people who came up with new concepts, medicine is now 100 times as much information in only 130 years since my grandfather's day. Now, wouldn't it be wonderful if that could happen with spiritual information? And I think it can.

PSD: Yes. Do you feel like you're just hitting your prime in your 80's here? You've never been happier?

SJT: That's right.

PSD: Do you have any fear in terms of your own mortality?

SJT: Yes, sure. I wish I didn't have to be so concerned.

PSD: Woody Allen once had a great line, "He had no fear of dying. He just didn't want to be around when it happens."

SJT: (Laughs) I like that. Me too...

PSD: Lastly, how would you like to be remembered?

SJT: Simply that I was useful, that my life had a purpose.

Mike Reid

"One of the things that drives me so hard is that this is not a rehearsal — this is the show, this is life. I may be tired, and my back may be hurting, but these are conditions I fully accept. Life is not meant to be enjoyed, it is meant to be experienced."

Songwriter and Composer.

Backstory: Mike was extremely reluctant to participate in the book but once he finally relented, we ended up talking for hours and running out of tape. After our official interview we connected several times for a series of the most fascinating conversations that truly opened up my imagination. Time after time I was blown away by the scope of his intelligence and his radical honesty. Mike is a deep and complicated thinker trapped in the body of an athletic icon.

PSD: You strike me as a very focused person.

MR: If I look back on the way I do things, I guess I am. I don't think it's an actual conscious decision where I say 'I have to focus now.' What I tend to do is take on things that are beyond me, that are beyond what my mind tells me I can do. Frost said, "One must begin on insufficient knowledge." It was exciting to hear that come from a great writer.

I think a sense of inadequacy is generally always there for me because you are always beginning on insufficient knowledge.

Elliot spoke of every start being a little failure. I'm not sure it is a little failure, but it is always a new beginning into places you haven't been before. So I always have the sense that the equipment is not going to be up to the task.

Another thing that factors into it is how my father raised my brothers and me. He used to say, "If you tell somebody you are going to do something, damn it, you do it." We live in a time where that is not really the case. But once you are raised that way, you never stray very far from it. By telling somebody, 'Yes, I will write this, I accept this commission to write this opera,' your mind is saying, 'you are an idiot.' But you proceed on insufficient knowledge, except the suspicions about doing it reside in the body.

PSD: Not in the mind?

MR: No, not for me. I walk around in this stuff and sense I have a notion of what the music should be. That is what you have to do. You need to focus, so you begin to understand your intent. Once you understand your intent, then it is a matter of rolling up your sleeves and moving the words and music around until you're really getting close to your intent.

PSD: Are you saying to begin with the end in mind?

MR: No, I don't think it's necessarily so pat that you can begin with the end in mind. I swear to you that is a challenge, that is a hard thing for anyone who wants to write. 'What am I intending here?' Writers of all kinds should write every day. They should think about walking around in this stuff even for ten minutes. It is using that part of your decision-making process, which is what I think writing is ultimately about.

PSD: Are you talking about the subconscious and the mysterious?

MR: You can't ever, ever consider writing without considering that. Because what I am trying to do — and what other writers are trying to do — is get into it. There is this neat little box called the ordered mind, the conscious mind, and the mind that says 'These are the decisions I make about who I am.' Well, baby, all this royal stuff underneath is too much a part of who you are to discount it.

PSD: An escape from the pragmatic mind to the unknown?

MR: I am 48 years old and I see it in my eight-year-old, who comes forth with stories, involuntarily. It's like breathing for her. My biggest job with her is to protect her imagination, to nurture this part of her. She is bringing it out of this place in the mind we're talking about.

Poets can get into this place. What is a little bothersome about education and socialization is that it's set up to protect you. Erroneously we say, 'We don't want these ions of original energy that the child brings into the world.

We want the child to get through life as painlessly as possible, and one of the best ways to do that is to act like everyone else.'

Fortunately, there are people who say, "I can't be like everyone else. I can't." They go off and write Beethoven's Fifth Symphony. Or they become Steven Spielberg or turn into Arthur Miller and Paul Simon. They just can't behave like everyone else.

There are also people who behave like everyone else far too long, then by the grace of something, realize it's not too late to discover the lost self. That's me. Then there are people who never address the ebbs and flows and pushes and pulls of their own impulses. They just continue to be like everyone else.

PSD: Inner success — the love of the process — is sacred. Like writing this book.

MR: The book is *Ashes From the Volcano*.

The volcano is personal and powerful to experience, but the thrilling thing is to see the ashes and expect something to happen. This human act of following what you expect to be the right course is a powerful act. When your suspicions prove to be correct, that is your reward. And it is a profound reward. It helps to further us along in the singular problem that all human beings have had, the search for who in hell we are. "Who am I?"

PSD: I sense in you some real change going on, some questioning on a very deep level.

MR: All this is imperfect stuff, but we can dig around and see what we can find. I mentioned the phrase, 'The recovery or the reclaiming of a lost self.' I grew up in Western Pennsylvania in a traditional working family. What you did if you were a kid like me was to be an athlete. I think there are some deep psychological things that go on with this. In some people, there are little alternative selves that you have to be kind to because they really are survival mechanisms. Jung talks about individuation, the point in life where you take the mask off and say, 'I am really going forth with me.'

I remember the first time I fell in love with a girl when I was seventeen. It was throughout the course of a summer. Of course, she was very cool about the whole thing. Then I went out on a Friday night in the first football game of my senior year and ran for 225 yards and scored five touchdowns, thus becoming 'big news.' A star was born. Before the game, I had asked if she was going to the dance afterwards, and she was saying, "Maybe I'll see you there or something." Then I have this big game, Dad gives me the car, and there is that girl mooning me with her eyes saying, "Can I go to the dance with you? I only want to be with you."

Looking back without too much analysis, a little war begins there. Football Mike says, "All right, everybody, listen up. I'm in charge from here on out. This feels way too good to let Mike The Writer call the shots. No one is going to screw this up." Football Mike was in charge, and football paid my way through college.

PSD: You won the Outland Trophy for being the best lineman in the nation.

MR: I was the Outland Trophy winner.

PSD: Did you work as hard in athletics as you have in writing?

MR: I was always working out to be in shape, but I have worked far harder as a writer. Writers work much harder than athletes. The most difficult thing in life are the choices one makes and being responsible for them. Athletes don't have to do that, they just have to get in shape and drive themselves. There is no choice to that. It is just an animal reacting to a stimulus.

That's the tough thing about writing. The opera that I wrote was an hour and twenty minutes of choices.

PSD: Are you ever satisfied with what you have accomplished?

MR: Hell, no! I remember a couple of years ago when somebody said, "Make a record. Here is some money, go in there and be yourself." It sounds inviting until you get in there and find out you haven't a clue as to who the hell you are. You need to travel through some neighborhoods where you don't belong to figure out and identify your self.

But you take a look at your stuff, your commercial success, the success you have had in the public sector. A hit songwriter is hoping to get the public's attention. I took a look at this stuff and I said, "All right, there is something missing. What is missing here from this work?" And I identified what was missing.

ME! ME!

One of the testicular density checks in life is being able to listen and pay attention to what your life is asking you to do.

PSD: Popular songwriting seems to me a lot like the jingle business.

MR: Hit songwriting is generally about a journey outward, away from the self, into the external world. When you have had success doing that, the tough thing is when life comes along and says, "What I ask of you now is to go inward." This means you may write more truly. You may write something that you find an amazing peace about, that you never had before. But you write at the expense of the audience. You may lose a lot of people.

PSD: More tough choices...

MR: As a maker of music, do you want to be a slave to the five million people who buy your records on their terms, or have an audience of 350 people that you are really connecting with?

PSD: Do the answers for you have to come through music, or can they also come through your children? Is it all funneled through the prism of your work?

MR: I have to work very carefully on that.

My children came into the world bearing huge gifts for my wife and me. We just listen to them and pay attention to them.

PSD: What do you feel is your biggest challenge right now?

MR: In an age of unbelievable technology where we are literally overrun with information and noise, one of the great challenges for me is to not stop caring about everything and to try and figure out a way to continue to stay engaged.

To not take this baby out of gear.

PSD: But is life really what we see on CNN?

MR: You know what the big information picture does? The most harmful thing it does is to destroy local culture. Local cultures used to exert a centripetal force. But we have all become part of feeding the big picture centripetal, so centrifugally it spins out to us the same books, the same CNN bullshit, the same Sylvester Stallone movies, the same, the same, and the same. Television does that, too. Something that you never see people do on TV is sit there and watch TV.

They are doing what we used to do, which is relating to one another. Shows like *Cheers*, where you have a little community of people telling each other their stories. In telling each other our stories, we knew one another. In knowing one another, we trusted one another. And when we trusted one another, we helped one another. We don't do that anymore.

PSD: How do you define success?

MR: I have no definition for it. I don't feel successful, I don't feel unsuccessful. The only thing that I have done that causes me to think that I am a success is that I am in control of my life. My life is not being pulled in any direction by someone else. I am in control and I am the architect of my life.

PSD: Do you simply love to create?

MR: When someone says, "I write because I have to," I

always think that is such a horseshit answer. That may be because I don't feel that way, and I insist that other people feel like me. That is always what arguments are about. You know the number one problem that my wife and I have? She just refuses to be like me. (He laughs.) I don't know why.

PSD: When you can obviously see what is right.

MR: Exactly. (He laughs.) Why wouldn't she want to be like me? She probably wonders why I want to be like me. We have been together for 22 years.

PSD: I'd call that a form of success.

MR: My friends who are divorced say that the overwhelming feeling they are left with is that they have failed. I don't understand that. How can you measure success or failure in interpersonal relationships?

PSD: Do you think our natural course of action is laziness or entropy?

MR: I always watch those nature shows, and really envy the Silverback gorilla whose only mission in the course of the day is to eat. I have never thought about it, but laziness is natural for me.

PSD: Was the 'real' Mike Reid a poet and a writer, born into an athletically-gifted body, who ended up on the gridiron as a sports hero through the natural inertia of cultural acceptance?

MR: I have only just felt that I could stand up and say that. And I said it to somebody out of frustration in an interview. Whether you like it or not, athletics was never a purpose. It was what I did on the way to discovering my purpose.

So the answer is yes. It's not an easy thing, at least for me, to stand up and say over the arc of my life, 'I am this writer of music.' It may be bad or it may be good. The quality of what you do is not the issue. Sometimes at night when I am really fatigued and most vulnerable, I begin to wonder if I don't really belong coaching a junior high school football team somewhere.

PSD: Is a deep sense of doubt what drives you so hard?

MR: Maybe so. One of the things that drives me so hard is that this is not a rehearsal — this is the show, this is life. I may be tired, and my back may be hurting, but these are conditions I fully accept. Life is not meant to be enjoyed, it is meant to be experienced. I look back over the 48 years of my life and say, 'It has been a good one.' But it has been a good one because I have put some effort into it. Something in me finds the natural impulse towards laziness to be completely unacceptable, particularly at my age when you discover that the most beautiful and valuable thing you have is time. What are you going to do with it? You can't choose the time in which you live; you can only choose what to do with that time while you live.

PSD: What would you tell your son if he was 18 years old today and looking for some direction?

MR: I would say, 'Pack up a few things in a bag. Take off and find out what it is that engages you, what resonates within you.'

That is the whole key to the rest of your life -- finding out what is sufficiently meaningful so that you can spend the rest of your life with it.

PSD: The beauty is that things can change. You are a

perfect example of that.

MR: I am and I am not. I don't put music into categories. I have often felt that if you really fell passionately in love with writing, you would write your way into obscurity. When you go down to places that you haven't been, the audience that knew an easier side of you is not going to want to go there.

PSD: But if you have enough money, who cares?

MR: That's the practical part to this. I have enough money right now. If I won the lottery, I wouldn't change anything in my life. I would give Mac Pirkle enough money to buy his own 400-seat theater. I do worry about my kids having too much.

PSD: That is a real challenge. How do you keep the well-fed hungry?

MR: What a great question! Have you ever said that before?

PSD: No, it is a wonderful part of the whole process of personal exploration manifested through the book.

MR: "How do you keep the well-fed hungry?" is a really great question. It feels like there are some rather vacuous forms of entertainment that are generating huge sums of money. The reason they are generating these sums is that people pay to see them. I think it is curious how we as a culture seem to need these empty, vacuous forms of entertainment.

I haven't figured out why this is. America has never been excited about the inward journey. But we are finding out now that the alternative is not working. There is a pervasive sense of dissatisfaction across the country.

PSD: Are you a spiritual person?

MR: Belief-wise, what makes sense to me is my belief in God through the divinity of nature. One of the disadvantages as a human is to look out there and see that the tree is crooked and think, 'That tree should be straight.' I look up at the stars and go, Ah!' You encounter art in the same way. You encounter Brahms in the same way. You think what a wonder this is.

PSD: Do you have a spiritual center?

MR: I have almost come to a place where I think if we can know our spiritual center, then that is not it. God, art, and love are things we cannot know. We insist on knowing them, and I think that insistence gets us in trouble. We can't know these things. Jerry Falwell might say that I will burn in hell for saying that I cannot know God. But I believe that the most you can do is experience these things and then wonder about them.

I have pain like everyone else, but middle-age has brought me to the place where I find it less and less necessary to make the pain go away. The difficulties of life are what life is. We continually make moral judgments about things, where nature does not. Nature just is.

Identify the questions that mean something and embrace the question. The best we can do is to live the question. If we live long enough, and if we live the question truly enough, we might live our way into an answer or two. The necessity to know things that are unknowable only creates sadness, frustration, and unnecessary heartache. Life is difficult. We must accept that.

PSD: Do you believe the inner part of you is connected

to something transcendent?

MR: The inner part of me is absolutely connected to something bigger. I don't believe that I am going to come up before God, and he is going to go down a list of bad things I have done, and say, "I'm sorry, you can't get in." The assumption that you were born bad — original sin — is a bad way to begin this whole thing we call life.

Pat Summitt
(New 20th Anniversary Content)

"One of the things that drives me so hard is that this is not a rehearsal — this is the show, this is life. I may be tired, and my back may be hurting, but these are conditions I fully accept. Life is not meant to be enjoyed, it is meant to be experienced."

Pat Summitt was the head coach of the University of Tennessee Lady Volunteer basketball team and is now "head coach emeritus." At the helm for 38 seasons, she is the all-time winningest coach in NCAA history for men and women teams. She is forthright, well-respected, ethical, and a winner who serves as a shining example in the sport of collegiate basketball. On August 22, 2011, Summitt raised the bar on courage as she bravely revealed the toughest opponent she will ever have to battle, early onset dementia, and Alzheimer's disease. She passed away on June 30, 2016.

Backstory: Through the help of some friends, I was able to arrange an interview with Pat on her visit to Nashville. The funny part was since her day was so busy, we did the entire exchange as she was driven around town between events. We sat in the backseat and the tape recorder was between us. Pat was warm and funny, but you could also feel the incredible intensity that burned within her. The woman was a force.

I also got meet her husband and it was interesting to see how she could shift gears from coaching icon, to fun, loving partner without missing a beat.

Her intellect was formidable, so I felt great sadness when I learned of her suffering with Alzheimer's disease and what that does to one's mental abilities.

PSD: How did you get started in coaching?

PS: Well, when I was a senior in college at the University of Tennessee at Martin, I tore my interior knee ligament. So I just started thinking about what do I really want to do? I thought I would go back home and coach and teach. I really teach. I hadn't thought that much about coaching, and then I realized how much I loved the game when I didn't have it. So I think it just really motivated me to go into coaching. Also, I really love working with young people. I love kids. Now I was pretty shy at that time and didn't know about teaching. But I thought well, you're simply going to have to do it.

PSD: Was it hard as a woman in those days and did you run into a lot of roadblocks just because of gender?

PS: It was out there but I didn't know it. You know, I didn't live it until I went to college and then I saw it. We had no scholarships and a $5,000 budget for six sports. And the girls played in the old gym and the guys played at Stokely and that's when I thought, "Wow, why?" We didn't even charge admission. It was really just a step up from the intramural level and it started to bother me because I just knew it was unfair.

PSD: This game has been a huge part of your whole life.

PS: Well, it's like the game of life. There are a lot of similarities. I didn't know my career would go down the path that it has, and I had no way of knowing because at the time you couldn't look at it and think there could be anything bigger than what it was then. I've just been really fortunate and really blessed. And I'm appreciative and think it's so important for kids to participate in athletics, because you learn so many valuable life skills. At the time I didn't realize what I was getting into, but now I understand it.

PSD: Talk about some of those game skills that are transferable to the way we live.

PS: Well, I think to be good at anything you have to have discipline. I think you have to be able to keep your focus on what is really important and what it takes to get to that level. You have to not only start the job, but also finish it. I think you need a real work ethic because you can really outwork people. I found that out a long time ago. If I'm not as talented as you, I can still beat you because I'll outwork you. Now that doesn't always win out against people that are gifted and willing to work hard themselves, so you have to work smart.

PSD: Were you raised this way?

PS: I think that it comes from my working on a farm. My dad, I mean he really just put us all to work. He had hired help, but he also had free help. He had all his kids on the farm working. I didn't realize it at the time he didn't pay us, but he was really paying us. He taught us a lot about just preparing for life.

PSD: How would a young person cultivate that work ethic?

PS: Well, I think first it's just realizing, if you set goals and if you aspire to reach those goals, what goes along with it. You have to go out and make the commitment, do whatever is necessary to achieve those goals, and usually that's related to hard work and there's really no way around it. If you have homework, it's not going to get done unless you do it. Just like our son with his chores. I mean, it's easier for parents to do it for their kids, and a lot of times it's easier for me to go ahead and do something instead of requiring the people that I work with to do it. Getting the student athletes to maybe go out and work, speak at the community or whatever they need to do. In the end, I think you just have to make people accountable. It's just roll up your sleeves and go do it. Don't procrastinate.

PSD: There's also a great joy and satisfaction in the actual process not only in arriving at the destination.

PS: Yes. I love the process and I'm always telling our student athletics that we're going to work hard but we're going to enjoy the process because in the end the results will be so rewarding and so much fun that you'll forget about the pain in all of the work. There was someone who compared it to having a child. It's intense labor. It's a lot of pain, but once you see that child you forget about the pain and you see the beauty of the results.

PSD: What's it like for you being a mother to your son Tyler?

PS: I've often said that he's taught me a lot more than I've ever taught him. He would probably agree with me. (Laughs) We're learning everyday and he starting to get really curious and asking a lot of questions. So now I really have to be on my toes! But you know, it's the greatest victory in my life. There's no question, I just feel like it's a gift from God, and it's important to help him everyday to understand life and to learn life skills. That's what it's all about. You want to love them, but it's important that you teach them. They understand right from wrong. I think he understands it, but we've already talked to our son about peer pressure, even as a 9-year-old.

PSD: Was it hard to shift gears from being the high-powered coach to the loving mom?

PS: Yes. And I think it was actually good for me. I think you learn a lot of things when you have a child of your own that I'm not sure you can learn from being a teacher or a coach, because you're with your child everyday. You go home with them and get up with them. You realize just how fragile they are and how sensitive. And when they're young, how needy they are. And then you also recognize you need to start teaching them to be self-sufficient by seeing firsthand just what it's like to be helpless and that fragile. Then I think you realize the depth of love and understanding and teaching and nurturing that it takes to have a child. So while I'm working with older kids, I still think a lot of that applies. I see they need a lot, too.

PSD: It's easy to define winning on the court. How do you define winning in life?

PS: Well, I think for me it's about making a difference. Actually, I think probably first and foremost, it's about being happy and what makes you happy. You know, for some people it's recognition, it's money, it's a title. For me, it's all about people. I love people and I like to make a difference, particularly for young women. And I think too it's being able to go out and compete. I love competition. I really do. It just so happens that basketball is the platform that allows me to really go out and compete. But I'm not the one playing the game, so I'm really preparing people for competition. And I think that's a carryover from loving to compete myself. I just always want to keep score. (Laughs)

PSD: With all this energy going out, what do you do to nurture yourself from the inside?

PS: Probably not enough. I go home and cook. Cooking is an outlet. Jogging is an outlet for me. And usually during the season I do a bit of lifting, too. I really started to enjoy that and sometimes just being at home.

PSD: So do you take quiet time? Do you meditate?

PS: No. My faith is important to me. I grew up in a disciplined home. But also our faith was important, and we still go to church when we can.

PSD: But you can find grace everywhere?

PS: Oh sure. And you know, to me you don't have to go to church to connect with God. You can pray every day and we do. Certainly for me that helps keep me grounded and gives me strength.

PSD: And a lot of people and a lot of leaders are afraid to talk about their beliefs or God. And it's a shame because I think that's such a powerful part of success for a lot of people.

PS: You know, it is. But I think I understand that and I'll tell you why. Because I think people have been criticized for trying to influence young people in a very particular direction with Christianity or a specific religion. That came up when I started coaching and teaching. And that was something that you just didn't do. I would say our team as a whole is very strong in their faith, and yet we don't talk about it a lot. We may talk about it one-on-one. If you look at prayer in school or in athletics and there's been real problems with coaches who wanted to have prayer before competitions. You know, it hasn't exactly been a situation in which people in our profession felt comfortable.

PSD: Have you adjusted to becoming a celebrity?

PS: There's a responsibility that goes with it. I've known all along that I was a role model, but I think you're even more aware. You think you have to be accessible to the public, but at the same time, I think you have to keep things in perspective and know that you can't be there for everyone all of the time. It's been humbling really for me, because I don't know what I said today at that event to all those kids. Every now and then Henrietta comes out in me. (Laughs)

PSD: Who is Henrietta?

PS: That's where I grew up. I don't know what I said. I was working on my speech and Henrietta popped out. But I grew up in the country and I'm proud of it. It's so much of who I am. I guess it really bothers me when people get the big head or think they're better than people because they've been successful. They've been blessed – so very blessed. So I think I have a feeling, a desire for giving something back. I want to give back, and that's my way of sharing what I think has been a gift for me. I think I have a special gift and I don't want to ever take it for granted.

PSD: It really is a tremendous gift.

PS: Really, I'm telling you. You're talking about someone that, (she points to herself) I mean my husband RV couldn't even come listen to me speak when we first married. I was too self-conscious. I was too unsure of myself. One thing I would say is writing the first book has probably changed me as much as anything as far as my self-esteem and my confidence in accepting who it is I am. People would always write about how tough I was and how demanding and they viewed me as being mean. I never thought of myself as being mean.

PSD: If you're that tough on other people, how tough are you on yourself?

PS: I'm pretty tough on myself. You know, I am really tough on myself. I've been really hard on myself lately, just trying to get these kids ready and thinking, no, I've got too much going on. I need to settle down and focus. When they have a bad practice I'm the first person that I blame.

PSD: Are you a perfectionist?

PS: On certain things, not everything. But I am as a coach. I am as a coach, I really am.

PSD: Haven't you gotten easier on yourself through the years? Have you been able to accept yourself for your strengths and weaknesses?

PS: Better for sure, I think, with age and, of course, Tyler.

PSD: I would think motherhood would probably soften you.

PS: Oh, it has tremendously.

PSD: And I bet that's made you a better coach and probably a better person.

PS: Oh, I think, no question. No question. You feel things you never felt in your life when you become a parent. It's truly had a very positive influence on me personally and professionally.

PSD: What would you tell Tyler if he was 18 and ready to go out into the world on his own?

PS: Make good decisions and make good choices. I would remind him of the things we're always teaching him. You're in control of your life and you have so many choices and you need to carefully think about how every decision will impact you or the people you're with or your family. Also, I would let him know we'll always be here for you. We trust you, we love you, and we want you to grow and be independent. But we want you to know you'll always have us if you need us. Always.

PSD: How do I make good choices since that's the key?

PS: Well, there's a right and a wrong way to do things. Always do what's right. Don't ever operate in the gray. You've got a set of standards. He has principles that he's been taught and he believes in. Don't ever lower your principles to accommodate someone else. Because, in the end, you're the one that will suffer and you know that's not right.

PSD: Does the heart tell you what to do in that case? Go with your heart, listen to your inner voice?

PS: No. Your heart doesn't always tell you. That's the times you really need to think with your head. Your heart might get you in trouble.

PSD: Is it hard to let go of some of the girls and move on after four years?

PS: You know, it's really not as difficult as you think. I guess when you've done it as long as I have, you just understand that's part of the process.

PSD: You've had a 100% graduation from your four-year players. So you really stress the academic, obviously. There's no bending of the rules sort of thing.

PS: You wouldn't want to be the first. So they keep it going. Peer pressure right there.

PSD: What challenges do you see, from your perspective, that a college student athletic faces at this point?

PS: God, there are so many.

PSD: With all the money being made from athletics, shouldn't these student athletes be getting paid?

PS: Well, yes. I think they should at least give them some spending money.

PSD: A lot of these kids are so poor, you know, a few hundred bucks here and there is for them a lot of money.

PS: A lot of money.

PSD: And what about the time demands? I mean, nowadays, in some of the programs, the word "student athletic" is almost an oxymoron.

PS: The NCAA tries to police that because they have a 20-hour rule. So, to some extent, that's still 20 hours a week plus going to school.

PSD: How many years have you been married?

PS: 19!

PSD: For you, what makes a marriage successful?

PS: I think you have to be good friends and I think you have to respect each other. RV is very supportive of my career. I think obviously today there are more two-career families. But I think it's just the fundamentals of our relationship. You know, you need love but you need friendship and you need to be able to talk things out and not be in competition. One thing I would say to parents is I think it's so important that, even if you have differences about how you want to raise your children, that when you talk to your children, you talk to them in one voice. Then you're both on the same page, so there's no confusion. I think that's so important.

PSD: Talk about the magic of love in all things you do and life.

PS: I think it's just, you know, it's passion...

PSD: Yet it's magical.

PS: Yes, it is. For me I loved life as a kid. I just really want to enjoy each day. I don't think that I realized how much I loved basketball until I didn't have it. One of the best things I did, I worked for United Way and I co-chaired a $7 million campaign and I went to several of the over 50 agencies there in Knoxville. I saw all kinds of needy people and all kinds of handicapped people, and it just had an incredible impact on my life. I've always been around healthy people. In fact, my family has all been healthy.

PSD: Athletes are usually in peak condition.

PS: Yes. I've never been around people that just are really having struggles where they were either mentally or physically retarded or had been in serious automobile accidents. And it just made me realize, it's humbling and it makes you aware of how truly blessed you have been. But it's funny that those people, when you just look at them, it's amazing they just always seem to be smiling.

PSD: Please share that story about seeing the guy in the South of France.

PS: We were in Nice and we were out walking, just power-walking the day before we left. I was just thinking about everything and you know a schedule can take you over. Or I'm overwhelmed and thinking how important basketball is and we've got to win and I hope those freshmen are good. So here I am, with all of these thoughts, and we turn around and I see this young man in a wheelchair with no arms and no legs. He's driving with the nub of his right shoulder with a little remote and he's got this pleasant look, he's got a smile. Man, it just hit me. We didn't say anything for a minute and walked on for a few minutes. So then I'm just thinking the whole walk back, "How could you ever complain about anything?"

PSD: Sometimes I feel like God is almost putting people like that in our path to keep our trivial concerns in the proper perspective.

PS: Yes. It's like, wait a minute, Pat. I thought, I wonder where that guy lives and I wonder if he comes out here every day?

PSD: He'll never walk on the beach and feel the water on his feet.

PS: No, he'll never swim. It's humbling and profound.

PSD: Where do you experience your deepest sense of satisfaction?

PS: I think being a mom and working with young people. I think, for us, it's having a chance to raise a son together and we have a great relationship with our son at this point.

PSD: I like the way you added "at this point" in case this comes out when he's a teenager.

PS: (Laughs) RV said, "You know I think we're really going to be good friends."

PSD: That's beautiful.

PS: Yes, and we've talked to him like an adult from an early age. You know, he always wants to come with us. He comes with me and sits on our bench. We have a packed house and he gets nervous. He gets real nervous, and I think it's good for him.

PSD: It's an interesting environment for a kid to grow up in.

PS: He thinks he's the good luck charm. I say, as long as you act like an adult, you can go with us anywhere. Sometimes he will go with us to black-tie events and I tell him, 'Now, if you go there and you act like a brat and you make a scene, that's the last time you go with us.'

PSD: You are teaching him personal responsibility.

PS: Yes we are. I said, I'm not going to make your decisions because I think it's important. That's one thing I've learned to do.

PSD: Do you think you're a better parent because you had kids a little later in life? At 21 you wouldn't have known all these things that you are passing on.

PS: You know, we waited a long time for Tyler and I think we've realized what a gift he was to us and I think we were old enough and financially in a position where we weren't struggling. We could enjoy (and have) the benefits of having full-time help. I think that made a difference. I really do and I think we were a little bit wiser.

PSD: What do you see yourself doing after coaching?

PS: I don't spend a lot of time thinking about what I'm going to do in 5 or 10 years from now. I try to enjoy every day. I think it's important to plan for tomorrow, but I think it's more important to enjoy today. Because, in the end, tomorrow may never come.

PSD: Tomorrow is promised to no one.

PS: Yes. I think the older I get the more I think about it.

I know we talk about planning and what we are going to do and when we want to retire. I've always said, 'well, I don't think I've painted myself in a corner.' I think there's a lot of different things I can do, and I think when the time comes I'll just know. I tried television, writing two books, but I'm not a writer. I think going out and speaking, I can do some of that. I will have to wait and see.

PSD: Pat, do you ever feel in awe of just the whole life show?

PS: Really, I love it, I mean it's fun. I feel like I've been really blessed and there's a story to tell because there are lessons to be learned.

PSD: How would you like to be remembered?

PS: Well that's easy – as a good person, as a good daughter, a good wife, a good mother, a good friend and someone who made a difference for others.

PSD: What does it feel like, in your heart, to make a difference?

PS: I think, when someone says to me, you know, I've really been struggling with my weight and now I understand I can do whatever I put my mind to. Or I've been feeling sorry for myself or I read your book and I went back and got my degree, any little thing. To have a player come back to me in 10 years and say I didn't realize what I was learning until I got out in the working world, the real world.

PSD: Those moments are the golden ones.

PS: Oh yes.

Thomas Frist

"I love people more than anything. The reason I practiced medicine is because I love people. I wouldn't give all the money in the world for the good things I did practicing medicine."

Founder, Hospital Corporation of America

Backstory: When I showed up to interview Dr. Frist he had no recollection of our appointment and was reluctant to share since, "I really don't have much to say or know very much." His humility impressed me immediately. Then he added, "Well, I can't send you away after you came down here to see me, so I guess we can try this, but please don't be disappointed."

After talking for two hours he invited me to stop by his home and meet his beloved bride, Dorothy. "Promise me you will come by sometime. Just drop by, we are always there in the evenings."

I came by and enjoyed their hospitality. Then became a somewhat regular visitor to their home. Though incredibly wealthy, they were humble people with a couple of older cars in the driveway and a great love of simplicity. They enjoyed watching the Atlanta Braves baseball games while eating TV dinners and regaling me with stories from their life.

Dorothy always said, "I could not live a day without Tommy," and he would smile then reach an old, trembling hand across the table and rest it on hers. He would then add, "She's the best thing that ever happened to me."

When Tommy was in the hospital I would visit him and we would chat about all kinds of things. When he discovered I was giving away the proceeds of the book to charity he told me, "I appreciate your generous heart, but remember that you have to take care of yourself and your family first, then give." He then informed me he was buying five cases of books to give as gifts.

On another visit to the hospital I was struck that this health care icon and the founder of a large chain of hospitals, including the one he was currently interred in, was in the end just another frail old man in a gown in a bed with needles in his arms. He confided he was tired and ready to go but he didn't want to leave Dorothy to live on her own.

One day I dropped by and found out that both of them were in the hospital. A week later, they passed away within hours of each other. Tommy first, then Dorothy. Sitting in the church at their funeral, looking at the two caskets side by side, I heard Dorothy's voice say, "I couldn't live a day without Tommy."

PSD: How did you come upon the idea to found a hospital chain?

TF: I was practicing medicine awfully hard, night and day, from eight in the morning to eleven in the evening. My only break would be to go home and see my children for an hour, maybe just to throw a baseball with them. I was also teaching medicine at Vanderbilt. Vanderbilt Hospital was always full, so was Saint Thomas — you couldn't get in there — and so was Baptist. So I said to four or five other doctors, 'Let's develop a small hospital for old folks because these other places always have a waiting period just to get in.'

We developed Parkview, which was a fifty-bed hospital and a hundred-bed nursing home. We designed it this way so if it wasn't successful as a hospital we could turn it into a nursing home. It was so successful we turned the nursing home part into a hospital.

One day, my son Tommy called me while he was in the Air Force as a surgeon in training. He said, "Daddy, when I come back let's start a chain of hospitals." I said, 'Son, are you crazy? You need to practice medicine.' He then called his mother and said, "I am going to do it anyway, even if Daddy doesn't help me." So the next day I called him back and told him I would help. We didn't have any money, so we got an investor, Jack Massey, who had a lot of money because he had recently sold his ownership of Kentucky Fried Chicken. Jack furnished the money for us to start HCA, Hospital Corporation of America, a name my wife came up with.

PSD: What inspired you to devote your life to medicine?

TF: My father died when I was eight years old. He was the stationmaster in my hometown, Meridian, Mississippi. One day he saw a lady holding a baby standing on the train track. She appeared to be hypnotized as the train was coming down the track. So he rushed out and pushed her off the rail. He saved the two of them, but he was killed.

We had no money at all, so my mother took in boarders to help pay the rent on our old three-story house. We had some interesting boarders, one of whom was a doctor. I went to work for him and he became my best friend. He was such a great doctor, I decided I had to be a doctor, too, because I loved what he was doing and I loved people.

PSD: You love people.

TF: I love people more than anything.

The reason I practiced medicine is because I love people. I wouldn't give all the money in the world for the good things I did practicing medicine. Helping patients was one of the greatest things in my life. I loved them and they loved me. I was always very close to my patients.

PSD: Why do you love people so much?

TF: I guess because my father died when I was so young and I missed him so much. Also, because my mother, who was so great, loved people. If you love people, they will love you. I just cared so much about every patient I saw.

PSD: Was anyone of great influence?

TF: My brother was by far the greatest man I have ever known. He was four years older than me. He was a father, a friend, and the best brother in the world to me. He died from colon cancer when he was only 50 years old but he helped me in so many ways. He was a minister and a great human being. I still miss him.

PSD: By all rights, you are a success on a lot of levels, so how would you define success?

TF: Being a good family man, working hard, and doing something for the good of people.

PSD: Why is family so important to you?

TF: Family means more to me than any thing in the world. In our family, no one has ever smoked a cigarette or anything. These are good kids. I have a good wife, especially as a doctor's wife, with me working every night. She was a great mother. She never complained at all. She gave all of her time to the children and me. You know, our son Billy came last and was a surprise. She was 40 at the time and I was 41. He was a big surprise.

PSD: That big surprise is a United States Senator now.

TF: Yes, Billy was the best thing that happened in my

life. He is a wonderful boy.

PSD: Did you have a philosophy as a father?

TF: I never spanked a child, I never cursed. I never did anything but talk to them and compliment them.

PSD: What advice would you give to a young man or woman to help them become successful — not only in terms of monetary reward but all-encompassing success?

TF: If you are successful, money will come naturally. But I wouldn't give my children money because I think they should earn it on their own. Money never meant much to me. I have given most of it away. I still drive a Chevrolet that is six years old. I never spend any money on myself. In fact, they say I'm pretty tight. But I was brought up to be careful. The two worst things in the world are having no money and having too much money. Am I talking too much?

PSD: Heavens, no. This is all about you!

TF: (He laughs)

PSD: What is one choice I can make that will bring me a deep sense of sustained happiness?

TF: That's an easy one. The most important thing by far is to marry the right girl. And I have been very lucky in this way. She has been a wonderful mother and wife.

PSD: In terms of a career or a calling, how does someone who doesn't know what they want to do, find that magical thing like you found?

TF: That is a very good question, but a very difficult question. If that doctor had not lived in my house when I was a boy, I probably would not have gone into medicine. My brother was a minister and I thought about doing that, but knew I couldn't give a sermon every Sunday. I wasn't smart enough. I am really street-smart but not very book-smart.

PSD: For all that you have accomplished, you don't seem to have a big ego. You come across as a very humble person.

TF: I have always had a very big inferiority complex, and in fact, I still have it. I can't walk in the doctors' lounge without feeling inferior.

PSD: Why do you think this is so?

TF: I don't know, but it's terrible. I never thought I was smart. I have felt inferior for a long time. In one way, I think it's good because when a person's cocky, it's one of the worst things in the world.

PSD: Do you think this inferiority complex may have been one of the things that drove you so hard?

TF: Yes, absolutely. I have worked really hard in my life.

PSD: It must be very challenging to grow old and have your body decrease in its capacity, especially with your mind remaining so sharp.

TF: You have no idea. I will tell you briefly about my illnesses. I was always healthy growing up, but twenty-five years ago I had a heart attack and almost died. I had to then have a heart replacement and had a second transplant eight years ago. I have had cancer of the colon and the prostate, but both were caught early so I am OK. I had a stroke during my first open heart surgery that paralyzed my right side. I got the movement back but I have trouble with my speech. I am also blind, deaf, and dumb! (He laughs.)

PSD: What keeps you going through all that physical adversity?

TF: My love of people and the joy I get in watching things grow. Trying to help people keeps me going.

PSD: Did you ever have any fear of dying during those hard times?

TF: Yes, I did, in fact often. But then Billy came down and stayed with me the whole night. He encouraged me so much that I didn't have as much fear. All my children were there for me. Having had two heart replacements is pretty rare, but I have had great doctors who have saved my life.

PSD: Do you ever feel like modern medicine is becoming too orientated towards technology and we are losing the personal touch that you so embodied?

TF: Sadly, yes. I don't think I could be a doctor now for anything because of all the changes, which are enormous. But the things happening in medicine are also remarkable. I used to see people die from typhoid fever and other infectious diseases, so there are incredible advances. Life will be lived a lot longer now.

PSD: What will be the most important thing you leave behind?

TF: My children.

PSD: What do you feel is your greatest challenge right now?

TF: Just to be alive and to stay alive. I also want to see HCA become a great company and continue to improve.

PSD: When you wake up every morning, do you feel that something as simple as another day is great gift?

TF: Oh, yes. I am 85 and should have been dead a long time ago with all the ailments I had. So I don't dread death at all. I just hope my death passes quickly and doesn't linger. I have had such a perfect, perfect, life. Nobody had a more joyful life or a better family. My life has been unbelievable. Losing my father and brother were the about the only real bad things in my life.

PSD: Why is it so important for you to give something back to the community?

TF: When you give back, you get back. When you give to people, not only with money, you get so much back. Medicine is a wonderful life to lead if you love people. And you have to really love people.

PSD: How would you like to be remembered?

TF: I told my preacher, 'Don't say too much. When someone dies, the preachers go on for thirty minutes or an hour. Don't do that. Just say he was a good man, a good father, and a good doctor. That's all.'

PSD: And he loved people?

TF: And he loved people.

Arum Gandhi
(New 20th Anniversary Content)

"I love people more than anything. The reason I practiced medicine is because I love people. I wouldn't give all the money in the world for the good things I did practicing medicine."

Arum Manilal Gandhi is an Indian-American sociopolitical activist, and the fifth grandson of Mohandas Gandhi through his second son Manilal. He founded the M. K. Gandhi Institute for Nonviolence hosted by the Christian Brothers University. This institute was dedicated to applying the principles of nonviolence at both local and global scales.

Backstory: Imagine my surprise when I discovered the grandson of the great Gandhi himself was living just a short drive away in Memphis. He graciously accepted my request and we spent a few hours together in enlightened dialogue.

PSD: How did you ever end up in Memphis?

AG: That's a question everybody asks me wherever I go. When we decided to start this institute and when I say "we", my wife has always been a partner in everything that I've done. We decided to start this institute to teach people what non-violence is about. Because most people have the impression that non-violence is only about conflict resolution, like civil rights for the African American people or independence of the Indians and yet, non-violence has a proactive component to it also and that's how to avoid conflict. It's one thing to resolve conflicts peacefully but it's quite another to avoid conflicts. So when we approached several universities with this program, this university liked the idea and they offered us hospitality so we ended up in Memphis.

PSD: Tell me about the institute?

AG: The institute is about teaching proactive methods of avoiding conflict. It's been our experience that many of the conflicts in individual situations arise from two main sources. One is our inability to deal with anger positively, and the other is our inability to build and maintain good relationships with people. We are so ashamed of anger that we don't even want to talk about it. Parents will not talk about it with their children; teachers in school don't teach us anything regarding anger. Generally everybody wants to avoid the subject altogether. So we leave it to each individual to find their own ways of dealing with this, and unfortunately, the only way we can deal with it is by abusing it because we haven't learned any other way. We tend to act in a moment of madness when we have just lost it and we do something or say something that sometimes changes the course of our lives completely. So what we try to teach them is how to avoid doing something when we are not in control of our mind, how to take time out and how to channel the emotions and the energy into positive action. We teach them how to write anger journals and write the journals with the intention of finding a solution rather than just pouring your anger out. It's not enough to just get the anger out of your system. While getting it out of your system, you also need to find ways in which we can resolve the issue that causes the anger. Because if we don't attend to that, then it's going to come back again and haunt you as long as possible.

PSD: How about in terms of the relationship aspect? What do you teach to cope with the conflicts that arise?

Basically, the capitalism system tends to make us selfish and self-centered. We only think about ourselves: we want to rise to the top, we want to earn the most money and so we do it by any means possible and that is a very selfish attitude, which translates in our relationships. All the relationships we have are self-serving. We must gain something out of it, and if we don't gain then we don't want the relationship. Now that's a very negative way of building relationships.

Now some of the school systems have started teaching tolerance, that we must tolerate people and that also is a very negative way. We don't want people to tolerate each other. We want people to respect each other. So we teach them how to build a relationship with the core principles of ideal relationship: respect, understanding, acceptance, and appreciation. If we respect ourselves and respect each other, then we'll respect our connection with nature and all of creation.

You know, we tend to believe that we are independent individuals and we can do whatever we like and it's nobody's business. But nobody is independent. We have inter-dependence and are inter-related, not only as human beings, but human beings and creation. And this is something important that we need to respect. When we respect that, then we understand who we are and what we are and why we are here. We have a role to fulfill. It's not just wiling away the time until we die and make the best of the situation. But we have a definite role to play and we can understand that role only when we understand our relationship with creation. So once we reach that understanding, then we reach an acceptance of the differences that exist between us. And then we reach an acceptance of our humanity.

PSD: That is beautiful and also fundamentally very practical.

Yes. So these are the principles that we try to teach in

these two main categories. We've been able to see a really positive effect from (of) this. A lot of people have begun to use it in their lives and they've been able to deal with things more positively than they used to.

PSD: Is it the ego that wants to be self-serving and selfish with a "what's in it for me" paradigm?

AG: Yes, it's the ego because, as I said, it comes down again to the society that we have built. We measure success by material possessions. A person who draws a salary of $70,000 is more successful than a person who draws a salary of $35,000. That's the criteria we use in everything. And so it boosts our ego all the time.

PSD: Yet any person on the planet with normal intelligence can know that everything material, including the body, is temporary. Yet the whole belief system in our culture is based on the illusion that you can actually acquire, own, or accumulate anything. Whether we know it or not, at best we are all renting.

AG: Exactly. Then on our deathbed we realize that we wasted all our time in accumulating all of this.

PSD: Yet people, for the most part, still do it.

AG: They still do it in spite of knowing that. And this is what we try to teach them: you know, it's not really worth it. I mean, we're not saying that you become paupers or just wile away your time. There are many more useful things to do in life than just accumulating wealth and money.

PSD: It seems people find out later in life, or in their last moments, it was the relationships they had, and the people they loved, that mattered most.

AG: Exactly. Most people on their deathbed always

long for more time with their families. If only I had more time with my family or my children or my wife or relatives. Nobody ever says, if only I had more time in my job.

PSD: What is your take on our compulsive consumption-based culture?

AG: This whole society has been built on materialism and it's a very young society. It's 300 years old and there is still a lot to see and experience in life as a society. So it's going through the phase of excessive materialism and someday the people will hopefully understand and realize that this is not all there is. Perhaps they will realize that we may have become a super power and the greatest nation in the world, but we haven't really gained anything out of that.

PSD: Yet for all of our wealth, we have yet to figure out how to keep our children fed.

AG: That is sadly true and very callous. Yet all of this is because of the lifestyle.

PSD: The epidemic of greed…

AG: And greed. The lifestyle generates greed. We've become such pawns in the hands of the producers, the people who make all this stuff and try to sell it to us. We are bombarded with this all of the time and the temptation is great, so we fall for the trap and go on buying things all the time. Then we just can't get out of it.

PSD: What advice would you give to a person to help them reconnect and recapture their essence?

AG: Well, I usually tell them they've got to take time out to slow down a little bit. If possible, remove themselves from their working situation for a few days and go into quiet seclusion somewhere and look inwards and try to put down on paper the things that are most important to you.

PSD: Most people in our society are terrified of the silence.

AG: Exactly. They don't want to look inside because they're so occupied with outward things. They don't want to look inside themselves. It's very important that we occasionally look inside and listen to our inner voice. When you put down on paper the things that are important to you and what you need to do to achieve those things, you would be surprised to find how few of those items will be dealing with material things.

PSD: You got to be with your grandfather, the great man of India, and spent some time with him. What was he like?

AG: He was a remarkable person. I'm always amazed at his capacity to deal with the most mundane along with the most important things. I lived with him between the end of 1945 to almost the end of 1947 and these were very crucial years in his life. We were on the verge of getting independence and also on the verge of being partitioned. So, in a sense, he was going to see the fruition of his dream and yet a destruction of his dreams, too. So it was a very crucial, very emotional and very trying time for him. But, in spite of all of that, he would spend an hour with me every day and just be a grandfather. Just sit with me for one hour, between 5:00 and 6:00 every evening, and tell me stories and just be jovial and laugh and joke with me and do all things that grandparents do with their kids. Then, promptly at 6:00, he would leave me and go back into his negotiations or talks or whatever he was doing. It always amazes me how anybody can do such things and switch from one level to the next level and come back again.

PSD: That's fascinating.

Also, he would never lose his temper. That was a very important lesson I learned from him. I grew up in South Africa, and I lived there for 23 years. At the age of ten, I was beaten up by some white students. Then, a few months later, I was beaten up by some black students. And both times it was because they didn't like the color of my skin. It became such an obsession with me that I wanted to be strong and be able to beat up the people who messed around with me. I started doing exercises and pumping iron to build up muscle and all of that. My parents decided I should go to India and live with Grandfather. The first lesson that Grandfather taught me was about understanding anger. He said anger is a very good thing, a really powerful thing, yet only if we can use it intelligently. But it can be really destructive if we abuse it. He used the analogy of electricity, and he said electricity is a very powerful energy. It's very useful if we use it intelligently but very destructive if we abuse it. But we channel it and bring it into our lives and use it for the good.

PSD: That's a great analogy.

AG: Learn to channel anger and use it intelligently so that we can find solutions to the problems.

PSD: Your grandfather often seems like the supreme example of human discipline.

AG: He was a tremendous disciplinarian almost to the point of being regimented. He would wake up at certain times and go to bed at certain times and do everything according to the clock and he expected everybody to do the same. Even fasting was a form of discipline for him because we get so hooked on eating and we want to eat all kinds of things at all kinds of time that we get ill about it. He would suggest to fast, to skip one meal a day for a period of time, or just eat fruit for a period of time. All of that was just trying to discipline you and so would be able to control your pallet and all your other urges.

PSD: Did he have a sense of humor?

AG: A tremendous sense of humor.

PSD: I had a feeling.

AG: A tremendous sense of humor! He was always cracking jokes and laughing and appreciating good jokes and good arguments, too

PSD: Do you ever feel any pressure to carry a name of such historical significance?

AG: No pressure. I mean some people foolishly expect things from you but then I don't blame the name or myself for it. But there are people with a very foolish attitude. For instance, and especially in India, when I used to be introduced as grand Gandhi's grandson, they would look at my size and say, "How can you be his grandson? He was such a lean person and you are so fat." (Laughs)

PSD: What do you think drove him, or drives any of us, so hard towards the truth?

AG: I think compassion and sincerity are the two driving forces.

PSD: Our soul wanting to do the right thing?

AG: If you have compassion then you'll feel compassion for people who are in trouble or who are in distress and who need some help. It's very easy these days to turn around and say, "Well, it's none of my business. Let them suffer with it." And that's what comes out of being selfish, self-centered. But if you have compassion then you feel like it's your business, and you want to do something about it. Sincerity is essential because, unless you're sincere in all your efforts, you'll never succeed.

PSD: Earlier today I interviewed Fred Smith, the founder of FedEx. We spoke about the fact that the world has enough resources. The problem seems more to deal with equitable distribution.

AG: Another lesson I learned from Grandfather all came about from a little pencil. A little 3 inch butt of a pencil. I looked at this pencil and I thought it was too small for me to use. I needed a newer pencil. So I just flung it into the bushes and I decided that evening I would ask grandfather for a new pencil. But instead he started questioning me and wanted to know why the pencil became small and why did you throw it away? Then he told me, you need to go out and look for it. I said, "You must be kidding! It's getting dark outside. How do you expect me to look for a pencil?" He said, "Well, let me give you a flashlight."

So I went out and spent about 2 or 3 hours searching the bushes for the pencil and I found it and brought it to him. He said, "Here are two important lessons that I want you to learn from this experience: The first lesson is that even in the making of a small thing like this pencil, we use a lot of the world's natural resources, and when we throw it away we are throwing away the world's natural resources. That is a crime against nature. Lesson number two is, because in an affluent society we can afford to buy all of these things in bulk, we buy it and use it indiscriminately. That means we are over-consuming the resources of the world and denying those resources to people elsewhere. That is violence against humanity.

PSD: That's a profound perspective.

AG: Indeed. Through that little pencil and this example I learned a profound lesson. Look at all the waste we encounter and all the things that we buy for no rhyme or reason. We don't need it and it's just because we have the capacity and resources, we go out and buy it. Then often discard it without a thought.

PSD: How can we change a paradigm like this?

AG: Well, I think if we change our attitude and we can become more compassionate and more sincere in our lifestyles. Then we will realize that many things we don't need, many things we can use again, and many things we can recycle and consume less. Then it just starts coming naturally.

PSD: It starts inside with us, and then we can lead by example?

AG: That's one of the mottos of my grandfather and one that we work on: 'We must be the change we wish to see.' In the end, it has to begin with each individual.

PSD: Because if not here inside, then where?

AG: Nowhere. We're always waiting for somebody else to start and nobody starts.

PSD: Are you a hopeful person?

AG: I'm always hopeful. Otherwise I wouldn't be sitting here with you or doing this work. I mean, in 7 years this institute has become nationally known, and that's a remarkable achievement. We're struggling for money and we don't have funding. We depend on donations and books sales and all of that. But we've come a long way. My wife and I were the only people involved in this and we couldn't afford to hire anybody. Today we have three paid employees and we have about a half a dozen work-study students and several volunteers, and this place is always humming with activity.

PSD: Things start humbly and grow in small increments and then reach critical mass. Your grandfather's work is a perfect example of that. Taking what would seem to have been something impossible, the British handing over India, and making it a reality.

AG: Yes, that's why Grandfather often said, "There's nothing impossible because everything that we once considered to be impossible is today possible."

PSD: On the human level, do you miss him?

AG: Oh yes, often.

PSD: Do you ever feel in your work a sense of him, a sense of his presence?

AG: Funny, I do feel that. I do feel very often when I'm puzzled for some answer to some question, it sort of comes from inside. I feel his voice and my father's voice, and my mother's voice, guiding me and telling me to do these things. When my wife does a lot of research, she goes through the 100 volumes of Grandfather's writings and a few times she's come back to me and said, "You talked about this in that meeting." And here I'm reading it for the first time.

PSD: A touch of magic.

AG: Yes, and I have not read all of those 100 volumes.

PSD: It's mysterious isn't it?

AG: Yes. I don't know, it's some inner voice.

PSD: Here you have this non-violent institute, yet both your grandfather and mother died violently. That must be terribly hard.

AG: Yes, we've had a lot of violence done to us as a family. But I haven't lost faith in non-violence because I still feel non-violence is the only way we can get rid of all of these violent acts, of the hate and the prejudice that we have for each other. I hope and pray that, perhaps one day, people will realize violence is wrong and that we need to bring about some change. I think we can see this happening. I just heard recently that the United Nations has passed one of the resolutions that I supported asking for the first decade of next century to be declared the decade of non-violence for children around the world.

PSD: That's historic.

AG: It is historic. And during that period all the members' states have requested to focus heavily on teaching people the value of non-violence at all levels. So I think that's a start. We need to try to change and perhaps that may make the next century less violent than this century has been. Sadly, this century has been the most violent one in human history.

PSD: Technology has afforded us not only great luxuries but great violence.

AG: We've killed more people in this century than we have in any other century.

PSD: Is it because we're so primitive that we are

inclined towards violence?

AG: Well, maybe not primitive. But you know Grandfather used to say materialism and morality have an inverse relationship. When you become too materialistic you become less moral. Then you begin to cut corners and take chances because you want to possess more and more. Ideally materialism and morality should be at the same level. Let's find a balance between the two. I think during the next century we are going to look for that balance.

PSD: How would you define success personally?

AG: I would say success to me would be how many lives have I been able to change and how many of those lives change for the better? Also, how many of them are going to genuinely feel sorry when I die, for my presence will be missed.

PSD: Touching people, touching lives one at a time.

AG: Yes, like Grandfather. Fifty years after his death, people are still mourning his death and saying why didn't he live a little longer?

PSD: This little old man in India had his teachings influence many others, some of them quite notable like Martin Luther King. He was a huge disciple of the non-violent method.

AG: I was reading the other day in a book a very important quotation. Somebody asked a Christian missionary, who was very close to Grandfather working in India, why didn't you ever attempt to convert Gandhi into Christianity. He was shocked and said, "What are you talking about? How can you convert a Christ-like figure? He was more Christ-like than anybody else I know."

PSD: The actual living of it and the being of it, that goes beyond any sort of dogma, creed, or color.

AG: Yet he respected all the different religions of the world. He said that nobody really possesses the truth and nobody knows what the truth is. We are all pursuing the truth and so, since we don't possess the truth, how can we say that one is better than the other?

PSD: Joseph Campbell, whose work I greatly admire, said, "The truth is one. The sages know it by many names. Did you think when you were young that you would be doing his work?

AG: No, never. It just came. And when I sit back and look at my life, very often the turns that it has taken are sometimes so totally random. It had never been planned. I can never say that I have exactly planned it this way and it was meant to happen. It just happened out of the blue. And I can't explain it in any way. In India I met Sonoma and fell in love, and we decided to get married. I couldn't come back to South Africa so I had to live in India, which was the first time and I think in many ways a very good time, because if I had gone back to South Africa, living in that cesspool of Apartheid I would have been a narrow-minded bigoted person.

Perhaps I would have wasted my life there. And I've seen many of my childhood friends who lived in South Africa, how they have become so narrow-minded because they were not exposed to anything outside. So leaving was a very eye-opening, a very broadening of perspectives and turns for me. Then we got involved because we were always so involved in compassionate things. We were never interested in material goods.

We barely earned enough for the family's survival. And so Sonoma and I used to spend time working with the untouchables and poor people trying to rebuild their self-respect and self-confidence. For 30 years we did that with very good results.

Many people have been rehabilitated, and programs are now going on and they have become self-sufficient because we empowered them and now they have been able to take over and move things on their own.

Then one day, out of the blue, an American came to India and she was sent to us by a friend who had met us earlier and told her that when you go to India you've got to go to Bombay and meet the Gandhi's. And she came and we had never met her before and we were sitting having dinner and just chatting like we are doing right now. She was very interested in the work that we were doing and we were talking about that. And suddenly it just occurred to me and I said, "Wouldn't it be an interesting thing to do a comparative study of the three types of prejudices that I have been exposed to?" In South Africa it was color prejudice. It didn't matter which race you belonged to; if you were not white you were black.

In India we have our own prejudices, a caste prejudice where people who look the same and have the same color and everything. But we found ways of oppressing them as untouchables and they lived in that oppression. Then here in the United States we have race prejudice, which is directed against one particular race and not people of color. There are a lot of people in that race who have lighter skin than I have, yet I am accepted more freely than they are. So I just expressed this. I said, "It will be a fascinating subject to study and try to look upon."

She asked me, also very casually, she said, "Would you like to do that?" I said, "Yes, but first I must get the financial aid and means because I don't have any money of my own." So that was the end of the story there. She went away, and then a couple of months later I get a letter from the University of Mississippi asking would you like to accept this fellowship to come here and do this study? That woman was on the board of the college in Oxford, Mississippi.

PSD: There's a beautiful synchronicity to this.

AG: Yes, but that's not the end of the story. Now that happened in '84 and we came here. Before we arrived here, the university told us, 'you buy your tickets and come in here and we will reimburse you for the tickets and all of that.' So we did, and by the time we landed, Reagan had cut the education funds and so our fellowship went with it. We landed and the university said, "I'm sorry, but we don't have the money to give you. Not even to pay for your tickets."

I had put all my savings in buying those two tickets for my wife and myself. So we tried to make the best of it. We stayed for about 8 or 10 months and got a few speaking engagements and all of that and got a few dollars for our expenses and then we went back to India. I couldn't go back and get my job again. We were trying to work our way through that dilemma for two years when again, out of the blue, Bishop James K. Matthews from Washington, DC called me in Bombay and said I had met him 35 years ago as a 16-year-old boy. So he says, "Do you remember me? I'm James K. Matthews, a good friend of your father's." I said, "Yes, I remember your name because I had a lot of letters from him to Father when he was alive." He said, "I'm here in Bombay, and I would like to meet with you and your family and make a connection." We were free that evening and he said, "Why don't you come over. I have some friends from America and we can all have dinner together." We went and had dinner with them and again, while talking after dinner, he was asking me what are you doing and all of that. I explained to him that this is what happened and we went to America and spent some time and we had to come back and we're in financial crisis because of that trip, but we were sort of picking up fresh and getting back. He looked very intense and he said, "Well, this is a wonderful subject to write about. How can we let a little money come in the way?"

He asked all the other people at the dining table, "What do you think, can we not raise $25,000 for this fellowship for one year?" Well, all those people at the table pledged $10,000 right away. And he came back to Washington and within a few months he got the $25,000 that was required, gave it to the University of Mississippi and we were back again.

PSD: Wow. Plus you were better for it in the way new relationships were forged.

AG: Exactly.

PSD: The universe moves in many ways.

AG: Yes, in so many ways. Now if anybody told me back at the beginning of 1984 that you'll be going to America, I would laugh at him and say, 'What are you talking about?' Yet I am sitting here today as an American citizen doing all this work and none of this I had any plan for. It just sort of came to me and something within me told me that I have to do this work and so I just started.

PSD: Does touching and working with people bring

you the most joy?

AG: I absolutely love it—especially with the young people. You know, they are the future leaders and I feel that if I can help them understand and change, then we can build some hope for the future. All these young people come here and come into our lives. And you know these last two days we were in LA and I addressed two meetings. And at each of them there were over 500 people and all of them were really touched. They didn't want to go home after that. They surrounded me in their talking and questioning me, and finally the organizers had to pull us out. That's been the response.

PSD: I find the truth is very powerful and exists way beyond the vehicle in which it is delivered.

AG: You know, Grandfather used to say that you must always look upon yourself as a farmer, and just as a farmer goes out into the field and he sows seeds and then he waits with hope and expectation that those seeds will germinate and he will have a good crop. It's the same way you go out and spread the seeds of peace and non-violence and just hope and pray that they will germinate.

PSD: It appears for you that everybody is really the same. It goes beyond the color, the creed, the religion, the dogma, the metaphors. It's just one brotherhood.

AG: Everybody keeps asking us about religion and do you teach religion and I say, "No we don't. That's private business. We don't want to get involved in that." Our doors are simply open. We don't ask them where they come from or what's your belief or anything. As long as you're interested in learning about this, you're welcome here with us.

Debbie Runions

"We in America have placed all of our eggs in the materialism basket, but I have never been materialistic. I have always believed that success has more to do with how much people love you, how much you are able to love other people, whatever it is that you have done to uplift mankind."

Educator, Member of President Clinton's HIV Advisory Council

Backstory: I met Debbie through my dear friend Jana Stanfield. She was a humble woman with a warm heart and sly sense of humor. At the time Debbie was openly advocating for AIDS awareness and was courageously sharing her story around the country. We used to sit for hours at her small apartment and over cups of warm tea, share our thoughts on the ways of the world. Her health at times was precarious but she would always find some wellspring of strength and rally back from the brink. Until the time she didn't...

I was so saddened by her passing but I often took comfort in this interview and Debbie's absolute knowing that mortal life was simply a stage on our never-ending journey of love.

I miss you my friend.

PSD: Tell me why you see yourself as successful.

DR: Because I have always had a plan, and definable, achievable goals. I come from a family that requires perfection, which is dysfunctional. So what I had to learn as a child was that you set goals you could achieve.

That way, you could see yourself as a success. What I said was 'I'm going to graduate from college;' then I did. Or 'I'm going to be a writer — not a famous writer, just a writer;' then I did that, too. If people assigned me something to do, my goal was to get it done and be on time. Because of these goals, I became a successful writer with a reputation as a person who could get things done.

PSD: What kinds of pieces did you write?

DR: Magazine articles. I wrote for Nashville magazine for eight years as a freelance writer. I am still a freelance writer. And I have a new book out called Sabrina's Gifts — it's a fairy tale about learning to fly by the seat of your heart.

PSD: Were you a natural public speaker?

DR: I learned to be one, because speaking is a terrifying thing to do. I didn't ever want to become a speaker. But after I became HIV positive, I realized that I was going to have to learn how to speak publicly. I hooked up with Jana Stanfield, a professional speaker, who helped me learn.

It wasn't as hard a leap as I thought it would be. It helped that I already knew how to structure a topic. The difference is that you try to be as objective as possible when writing, but in speaking, you try to pull people in, to get them to make an emotional commitment.

PSD: Talk about your life story, because I believe it will inspire people.

DR: The thing that makes my story different — in fact, my whole life story — is that my karma is immediate. The first and only time I had sex, I became pregnant. Oddly enough, we didn't even know we had had sex at the time. We didn't know we had done anything wrong. But within two weeks I said, 'Harry, I'm not feeling well.'

PSD: How old were you at the time?

DR: Seventeen. This was middle Tennessee in the '60s

and nobody talked about sex, because they didn't know anything to tell us. When I was 15, I remember reading this article in True Confessions magazine at the beauty shop, because Mama wouldn't allow such trash in the house. (She laughs.) It said "They kissed, and she got pregnant." So in my mind, you got pregnant through kissing. I asked this girl on the school bus, who knew more than me because she was 16, if this is how you got pregnant. She said, "No, silly, a boy has a seed and he plants it inside the girl and this is how it is done." I wondered out loud what this seed looked like. She said it was clear and about the size of a pumpkin seed, but no one had ever seen it. So I figured if I just stayed away from clear pumpkin seeds, I would be fine.

When the doctor said I was pregnant, I said 'That's impossible. I'm a virgin!' This is when my life of suffering started. We got married, and I went from a life of privilege to a place of poverty. Then Harry was in an explosion and almost died. A year later, he was in another explosion. It was a series of events I call suffering. I had to learn how to be happy amidst all of the tragedy. You can't let all this junk drag you down. We went to college, had kids, held down jobs, and lived on $250 a month.

PSD: After all those close calls, Harry still died young.

DR: In 1980, at age 32, he died in a car accident leaving me with two kids. Something else to overcome! Then my father died, my father-in-law died, my mother developed leukemia, and my stepmother, who was one of my favorite people, got Alzheimers. I lost her even before she died, a piece at a time.

All of this prepared me for my diagnosis of HIV. I had

already learned that you can't base your happiness on people, on money, or even on love. You have to find a center within yourself where you can find a sense of peace. Because I had already learned how to do this, the HIV coming along was just one more piece to overcome.

PSD: Life is hard, even without such dramatic tragedies. How did you come to find that inner peace?

DR: I'll tell you a story that might explain my foundation, and why it hasn't been as hard for me as it has for other people. My first memory was at my grandfather's funeral in October of 1953. In those days, they used to lay the body out in the front parlor. He was in the front room of Granny's house, and we used wooden Coca-Cola crates to climb up and view the body, since I was so tiny. I looked at his body and thought 'That looks exactly like Dad Fields,' but then looked into the corner of the living room and there he stood. I looked at him, looked at the body, then looked back at him and thought, 'Isn't that funny.' I got all excited because I knew my Mama was really upset. So I went to her and Granny, and said 'Don't cry. He is right over there in the corner!' They said, "Don't come to us with your Ellen Gordon stories today of all days!" (Ellen Gordon was the madwoman of the community.) At that point, Dad Fields put his finger to his lips. He knew I could see him, but it wasn't time to share just yet. So I have always known that death may have one appearance, but it is not real. Because my little three-year-old eyes could see what was real. The body was fake.

I have always been a very philosophical child, a spiritual child. They tell me I used to have conversations with people I couldn't see, even though

I don't remember this, and quoted scripture as soon as I could talk, but I wasn't taken to church until much later. In fact, Dad Fields used to say that I was a better preacher than any he had ever heard.

The other gift I have is the ability to detach and really observe. I also have a firm foundation in fundamental Christianity, which was a major hindrance for a while because it is filled with so much shame and guilt. But it gave me a foundation so that when Harry died, I had a rock under me. Then I found Unity Church, and after that, A Course In Miracles. I would say that A Course In Miracles has done more to help me find a place of peace than any other thing. That and the support group, Co-dependents Anonymous.

PSD: So you found that inner place that is separate from all the worldly suffering.

DR: Every single challenge comes with an equal opportunity for either blessing or tragedy. If you love somebody, that is a blessing. If that person dies, then it's a tragedy.

But it then opens up another door for new blessings. You just have to wait, and be patient that the blessings will arrive.

PSD: How did you contract the HIV virus?

DR: I got it from a man with whom I had a seven month relationship in 1989, someone I loved who was not a good person. I had broken off the relationship and we had been separated for two years when he called me. I spent one night with him, and that was the only time we had ever had unprotected intercourse in all of our relationship. There's that 'immediate karma' again — I contracted HIV that evening.

PSD: What made you come forward, and be brave enough to begin educating people about this disease?

DR: People see it as brave, but I don't see it that way at all. I have learned that we are only here for one reason and that is to learn how to love. I always ask 'What is the loving thing to do for myself and the world around me?' The loving thing was to speak it, because secrets make you sick. It is the shame about this disease that causes people to die before their bodies die. If someone with a high profile will speak out, then people on the street will get a clue that this is not a disease of street-people injecting drugs, or a disease of sexual preference. It is not a disease of people that are stupid, or people who do not care about themselves or the community. It's a disease that affects people.

PSD: Your involvement is a generous act, no matter how you look at it.

DR: I have always been told that I am part of a bigger community and that every man is my brother. Since there is no cure for AIDS, then the only thing I can do to help is to work with prevention. AIDS is almost 100% preventable, so it doesn't have to happen to anybody. Since teens are one of the fastest- growing at-risk groups, this is where I thought I could do some good.

PSD: How did you get started?

DR: I called the Center for Disease Control and said 'Surely you have money to do this.' They said the person in Tennessee to talk with is Elizabeth Word. I called her that day and she said "I am writing the grant this weekend, and I will write you in." The grant was funded and that is how I got the job. We sent out letters to all the schools in middle Tennessee and the response was amazing. Teachers are afraid to talk about AIDS because they might lose their jobs.

PSD: When you go out there what do you tell these kids?

DR: I tell them my story and how important it is to get your information from somebody who knows — not somebody on the school bus. I also tell them how to protect themselves. I tell them that I am not any different from them, that I come from a rural county like most of them do. I tell them that I thought I was too smart, but smart doesn't have anything to do with it. The children who come are amazing — they follow me to my car, saying that I am the first adult that has ever told them the straight truth. That I was the first adult to say they had sex before they were married. They are literally dying to communicate with an adult.

PSD: There's an ironic choice of words.

DR: HIV has forced me to become an adult. America is filled with adult children, people who refuse to take responsibility for themselves and their children. We have given our children away for other people to raise.

PSD: To TV sets and the streets.

DR: Absolutely. That's why we have gangs.

They're all lost children trying to find a family.

PSD: Like in the book, The Lord Of The Flies?

DR: Exactly. It's sad, yet it's a place where I feel like I can make a difference.

PSD: So basically you are out there telling these kids the truth. Do you ever get discouraged by the enormity of the suffering and ignorance you are confronted with everyday in the world? In some ways, you are like a cry in the wilderness.

DR: I do get discouraged. Sometimes when I go into schools these kids talk through my entire program, so I feel like I'm spitting into the wind. But then I get some wonderful letters from those same schools, so I guess somebody is (was) listening. One thing that metaphysics teaches is that we are just the instrument. God does the work, we just have to be there.

PSD: Have you run into much opposition from the religious right?

DR: Yes.

PSD: I would imagine that part of the problem is a high level of denial and the refusal to talk about the situation.

DR: Some schools place no restrictions. In others, you cannot even mention the word 'condom.' You have to say 'take preventive measures.' Some counties won't even allow someone who is HIV-positive to come into the schools.

PSD: Fear and ignorance?

DR: Just plain fear. My message is actually one of abstinence. However, if you are one of the majority of teenagers who are going to have sex anyway, this is what you need to do to protect yourself.

PSD: What reaction did you have when you first got the news that you were HIV-positive?

DR: Initially, I was depressed, which understandably is what happens to most people. Then I went into a period of elation because at last I knew what I had been preparing to do all my life. I knew how to write, I learned how to speak, I learned how to promote.

Now I have something to say.

PSD: What does success mean to you personally?

DR: The quote by Ralph Waldo Emerson you have in the front of your book. We in America have placed all of our eggs in the materialism basket, but I have never been materialistic. I have always believed that success has more to do with how much people love you, how much you are able to love other people, whatever it is that you have done to uplift mankind, to raise the consciousness of humanity, and knowing your own integrity and living it consistently. And I have done all that! The nicest thing anybody ever said was when my daughter wrote this letter that won us a trip to England. She said, "People always want to know what love is. I look at my mother and I know."

PSD: That is beautiful, and that is success.

DR: Yes, I was successful raising my children. I can't sew or cook, but I have been a good friend. If you can be a friend to yourself and the people around you in the world, then you are a success.

PSD: You met President Clinton. What was that like?

DR: What a HOOT! When I went to Washington for the first time, I went up to Al Gore and said 'You probably don't remember me, but I...' and he said, "I know you!" Being on President Clinton's HIV/AIDS Advisory Council is fun. It's the most diverse group of people I have ever met.

PSD: What was your impression of the President, does he strike you as a sincere person?

DR: He is very smart and very spiritual. He is sincere,

but he is splintered in many directions. I'm impressed by the people he has around him. He's a person who cares. He has a photographic memory and never forgets your name, even if he has only met you once. I feel very comfortable with him as President. The best thing about him is that he's flawed, so he has compassion. And I think that compassion shows. Clinton seems in touch with his feminine side and is able to communicate his feelings.

PSD: Right now what is your biggest challenge?

DR: This may sound petty, but the thing that drives me crazy is my time seems to be passing at light-speed. So I want everybody to be on my time clock. I have chaos going on in my body, so I need to have serenity and resonance around me. Now I have a daughter for a roommate who is not very orderly or on my clock, so this is very challenging. (She laughs.)

PSD: The small things are challenging you in the moment.

DR: They make me crazy, because they're the only things I have any control over. I have no control over the big things.

PSD: In the end, like all of us, you are being challenged for total surrender.

DR: I just can't give it up, though I do believe my daughter will force me into total surrender. (She laughs.) I am probably the biggest challenge in her life.

PSD: So your challenge is really about control.

DR: And it always has been. 'I've got plans, God. Let me do it!!!!' (She laughs.)

PSD: How do you feel about life?

DR: I love life, but I don't fear death. I was speaking with some second-year medical students and told them that I wanted to see them get out of the mode of being mechanics and become healers. And the only way to do that is to see death as a friend and not the enemy. Sometimes death is the healer. I love life. But I love life since HIV, and I think that is why HIV came to me. What HIV has done is given me focus and allowed me to be brave. Because of the changes in my life, my children's lives have gotten stronger and more directed. So I love life now, but I am also ready to move on.

PSD: How is your health today?

DR: Good today, but it comes and goes. I'm on steroids, so that makes you feel like you can play football. I feel OK, but I get tired very easily.

PSD: Since we have such short lives regardless of HIV, what would you tell someone about how to find peace and serenity in this life?

DR: It's a short life in some ways and a long life in others — when you're not feeling very happy. I would say, 'Follow your bliss. Find out what your passion is and follow it.' You have to find meaning. A book that changed my life was Man's Search For Meaning by Victor Frankel. It doesn't matter what your circumstances are, you have to find a meaning to be alive.

We need to learn that we are all children of God, and God cannot be whole without us. I discovered that our only goal is to learn to love and learn to be loved, and even if we fail at that, God loves us and grace makes up the difference. You come so far and grace carries you the rest of the way. If we could give ourselves a break and stop being so urgent in our doing and learn how to be, we could be happy.

PSD: How would you like to be remembered?

DR: I can tell you what is on my tombstone.

PSD: You already have it picked out?

DR: When Harry died, I bought mine, too.

It says, 'Friends.' Harry and I didn't have a passionate love, but we were best friends. I want to be remembered as 'People's best friend.' I hope my daughter and my son will say this about me. I know Harry would. So would the people in my circle. I would like for God to say "She was one of the best friends I had on earth."

Fred Smith
(New 20th Anniversary Content)

Frederick W. Smith is the founder, chairman, president, and CEO of FedEx Corporation, which is currently a $58 billion global transportation, business services, and logistics company.

Backstory: Everyone told me that the famed FedEx founder never, ever did personal interviews. So I was honestly quite shocked when he accepted. His people told me I would be given twenty short minutes and that was it. Fred was a little cautious at first. But as the interview progressed, I could tell he was not only feeling more comfortable but actually enjoying the exchange. We ended up talking for over an hour. Afterward, he graciously walked me around and shared some fascinating morsels of trivia or insights.

PSD: What does it feel like to draw up an idea on a little piece of paper, have a dream, and then to see it 25 years later become such a major, world-altering entity?

FS: Well, obviously it's very gratifying. My original idea was an academic study about the type of logistic system the computerized world was going to require and then the way to solve that logistics need was developed mostly during my service in the Marine Corp. So the coincidence of the original demand side and the subsequent supply side in the early 70's led to the founding of FedEx. I think it's been a reclamation of those original conclusions over and over again over the succeeding 25 years that has led us to where we are today.

This thing has become a very, very big enterprise. Yet to me, it's just a linear projection of the original premises. I'm surprised in certain ways, but on the other side of the coin I'm not so surprised because I was absolutely convinced that this was going to be a very big thing. I probably never thought that it was going to be this big. But I was always convinced that it would be a very large endeavor.

PSD: Did that faith and conviction, in the early years, keep you going through some very lean and humble beginnings?

FS: Yes. It was an absolute certainty on my part that it was going to work. And bear in mind that the trends were all in the right direction. It wasn't as if the company had gotten started and the progress wasn't continuous. It was. I mean, you could extrapolate forward right from day one that it was going to be successful given enough time and enough money to get to the critical mass. Though the delays in the original financing and the oil crisis of 1973 certainly threw some monkey wrenches into the spokes, so to speak. But it was clear every day that we operated, with the increasing acceptance of the service and the problems that it solved for our shippers, that it was going to be successful. So I never doubted.

PSD: Did you ever feel overwhelmed?

FS: No.

PSD: What innate qualities allowed you to do this?

FS: Well, I think there were several factors that were involved in that regard. First and foremost, I believed, as we've been discussing, strongly in the idea. Second, I tend to be very competitive to begin with, and I guess you could call that determination, but I just was not scared of losing. I just was determined to win. And then third, and most people who know anything about FedEx and know something about me also recognize that you've got to put my business experience in junction against my military experience. A lot of people in the business look at it as the end all and be all and I never felt that way. Dollars and sense are something. But compared to Vietnam, I mean, if you didn't make a success out of the business, it was pretty small in terms of the consequences. There are a lot of things that are a lot worse that can happen to you. So I think that was a big part of why I never feared failure—all three of those things.

PSD: How important to something like this is the process of getting and developing the right people?

Extremely. In terms of getting the right people, I do think that I have learned over the years and knew then too, although I know better now, the extreme importance of getting very good people, getting them to buy into the vision and then giving them a lot of authority and responsibility, working with them collaboratively and allowing them to make a mistake. Because if you don't do that you can never grow, and you can certainly never grow fast. This is because as you go up that growth curve, the tasks multiply not linearly but exponentially. So if you can't have them buy into a common vision, get lots of good people, and give them the authority to do things, you can't accomplish big things. It's impossible.

PSD: You brought up Vietnam. You were young. What kind of impact did that have on you?

FS: Well, it was the defining moment of my life, far more than Fed Ex has been. It permeates everything. I think about it every day. I probably think about it every hour.

PSD: What do you think?

FS: Well, I think about a lot of things. I'm not sure I want to share them in a book. But it just put in perspective what's important and what's not important. Vietnam was a very grueling experience and the consequence of making a mistake in Vietnam was that somebody lost their life. So comparing a commercial business enterprise to those consequences, as I said before, is pretty small change. But that's why during the early days when we did have some delays and oil prices and what have you, I never panicked because, in relation to my experience in Vietnam, it wasn't a very big thing.

PSD: One is life and death and one is numbers.

FS: Absolutely. That's exactly what I mean.

PSD: Did that sort of profound experience change your whole perspective on life?

FS: I don't know that it changed it, though it certainly honed my perspective about life. I suspect that I was in the Marine Corp in Vietnam precisely because I had certain traits or characteristics. But the experience itself simply magnified those and solidified my views on a lot of things.

PSD: What is some of that perspective?

FS: Well, my core philosophy is as I described it: you have to keep business in perspective.

PSD: Right.

FS: I mean, it's the whole person, it's life as a whole that's the important thing. And whether you're successful in business or whether you're unsuccessful in business, or whether you're this or that, it's got to be put in the proper perspective in terms of ones entire life—life, death, that sort of thing. And that had a very big effect on FedEx.

PSD: Would that help you be a more balanced human being, even though maybe you were starting a company, like taking time for the family?

FS: Well, my priorities are my family and then the business and I don't know that I've always been successful about it. But I've always certainly had my priorities.

PSD: That's unusual in today's current corporate culture.

FS: Well, maybe it is, I don't know. I don't think it's unusual. Other people think it is because the people that folks write about are the ones that end up not taking time for their kids or what have you, but most of the people I know in the corporate world do spend a lot of time on their family.

PSD: You're a CEO and a parent. Your business philosophies probably have been written about, but what has experience taught you in regards to raising children?

FS: Well, I think the most important thing about being a better parent is to give the one commodity that you don't have any extra of to children, and that's your time. I think the second thing is you've got to provide them the best advice and structure that you possibly can. Also, instill in them some philosophy about life. If you can do those things, then I think you would be generally successful as a parent. If you don't do those things, I would almost guarantee you that you won't be successful as a parent.

PSD: How about giving them room to grow and even make mistakes, like you do with your employees?

FS: I think in my experience in athletics and the military I've been very team-oriented. I'm very focused on trying to get a group of people to focus on a common vision and then giving them a lot of responsibility to extend that as much as humanly possible. Allowing them to win, to share in whatever the team produces. Over the years we have done that religiously with our profit sharing, with our promotion from within, famous complaint procedure to guarantee fair treatment procedure, our huge employee surveys, the survey feedback action and on and on. There's a very, very common thread. From the day that FedEx was established to today, it takes every member of the team absolutely devoted to this common vision to make an enterprise like FedEx successful.

PSD: Who influenced you to help develop this philosophy?

FS: Probably my coaches and the people I met in the Marine Corp. My father was gone for a long time, all my life. He died when I was four. So I think my influences were mostly the athletic coaches that I had and the people that I worked for in the Marine Corp.

PSD: Are you a person who likes to challenge yourself in terms of learning, and or reading a lot?

FS: I read a lot. That's my hobby, along with tennis, after my family. I think reading is absolutely essential if you want to learn the lessons of history and what other people have experienced.

PSD: Is there a major difference, in terms of being an entrepreneur and building something from the ground up, and managing something as vast as this has become?

FS: Yes, there is. And I've been asked about that before about being an entrepreneur and a manager. I don't think they're mutually exclusive. Michael Jordan is a fabulous athlete and a pretty good businessperson. You have lots of soldiers who were very, very able soldiers and ended up being very good administers and executives. Dwight Eisenhower is a good example.

Now, you have examples of people who were exactly the opposite. Patton, perhaps, in the military, and some of the often reported stories of athletes who can't handle the money and what have you. But it's not mutually exclusive that you can be an entrepreneur and transition into being a good manager. Scott McNeely did it. Bill Gates did it. Tom Watson did it.

PSD: Do you ever feel like you just want to go start something new from scratch now that you have done it so successfully once?

FS: Well, I've sort of done that inside the company. I mean, FedEx is a much different company today than it was before, and FDX, of course, the parent company, even more so. So I have done that over the years on numerous occasions. I never wanted to simply start with a clean sheet of paper and go do something else partially because I have always felt enormous loyalty to the people who started the company and have worked with me, and I have looked at the company as a mission unfulfilled. So, until I feel comfortable with that, I don't want to go off and abandon them. And I certainly don't want to go off and abandon them to simply make money. I mean, you can only eat so well and you can only drive so many cars. I've wanted the company to be successful certainly for myself and for the shareholders, but I've equally wanted it to be success for the people that decided to make it a career.

PSD: You mentioned wealth and, in our culture right now, there's tremendous emphasis and importance on acquiring a lot of money. As someone who has done well in a monetary way, is it overrated?

FS: It is overrated and in many ways it's a great burden because it brings with it all kinds of things, which are very, very unpleasant. The greatest burden that it brings is for those who have a great deal of wealth that are never satisfied with any level of it. But most people say that's easy to say for someone who has a lot of money and I wish I had it. But it's something that does bring with it its own baggage in lots of different ways.

PSD: It doesn't solve every problem. If nothing else, it creates its own. I mean, it might solve monetary problems at best.

FS: Yes, it solves monetary problems, but it also creates many other problems. So you've got to keep it again in perspective.

PSD: You did this because you loved it and not because you're trying to get rich.

FS: Yes. And my experience, by the way, has been that the people who do very, very well financially are not people who start out wanting to do very, very well financially. It's because they do something that they like to do which ends up creating a lot of money for them.

PSD: Do what you love and the money will follow?

FS: Right. Yes, I heard General Colin Powell give a speech here in Memphis one time and he summed it up probably better than anybody I've ever heard. He told the officers around the country to find something that you are good at and something that you love to do, and if you find those two things, you'll be successful and happy. If you don't have one of the two, then you won't be successful or happy.

PSD: What would Fred Smith's own personal definition of happiness be?

FS: Well, I suppose it would be someone who is content with the hand that life has dealt them, and someone who takes pride in what they have done and who has, most importantly, the family unit that is supportive and pleasant. That would be my definition of it.

PSD: Speaking of family, as a father what would you tell your child to get more joy or resonance out of the experience of life?

FS: Well I told my kids, and I have kids that go all the way from 30 to 11, and as each one of them has gotten ready to leave home and go off to college, I've told them several things and it's been absolutely consistent. Number one, they should go and attempt to get the best possible higher education that they can. Don't go to the easiest place. Go to the best school that you can go to and get the best education, because if you do that you will learn more about life than you learned in all the preceding years that you've lived. Higher education is sort of the opening window on the world. The second thing that I've told them is not dissimilar to the advice that I mentioned a moment ago that General Powell has given people – find something that really turns you on that you like to do and it makes no difference to me what that is. I have one daughter who is a wildlife photographer in Jackson and a good one, and another one who's a terrific advertising and PR person, and another one who's a registered nurse and mother. They've all found(gone) their own path and I have other children in college now. So I think those two things are important. And then a third, to try to be a good person. Because we all have faults and we all have problems. But evaluate them and extenuate the positives and minimize the negatives and be a good person.

PSD: What brings you the most joy and a sense of fulfillment?

FS: Well, I love to see my children succeed and I love to see my colleagues succeed. I love to see people try to do something and then win. To reach whatever it is that they've been trying to reach. I get a lot of satisfaction out of that.

PSD: Going back to your model of giving people authority and decentralization, do you think it's possible that we could create something like that in this country on a political level?

FS: Well, I think that it's being created at the moment but the people in Washington don't understand it. I think that the growth of the Internet is going to fundamentally change policies. I think that politics changed enormously with the telegraph and the railroads. I think it changed again with mass communications in the 30's. Today I think the growth of the Internet is going to be very, very profound. It's going to democratize all kinds of issues that are today dealt with only by a small elite that get input from their campaign contributors or polls conducted by the news media. I think what you're going to see, like the referendum in California has shown, is a much broader participation along various issues. You're going to be able to vote, in essence, on a lot of issues that are framed by activists and then put forward to the elected representatives in electronic form. I think it's going to change everything.

PSD: Do you think that's positive?

FS: Yes. I think it's basically a positive. I think you've got to be careful about it. I mean, the Greek experiment with democracy didn't collapse because democracy turned out to be evil. It collapsed because the democratization of everything led to chaos. I mean the word ostracized comes from the pot where people could drop their white and black pebbles in. All you had to do was drop one black pebble in it and you could knock somebody out or whatever it was you were voting on. And that is, of course, where 'black ball' came from. And it was the concocting of the democracy in its truest form that created the problems with Greece. It's also why the people who (that) set up the United States, the founding fathers, didn't set up a democracy. They set up a republic to filter a lot of the common emotions which are hot and passionate.

So I'm not sure whether it's going to be a good thing. We're just going to have to find out. What I am sure about is that it's coming. You can see it and I think that will change things a lot.

PSD: Are you an optimist?

FS: Yes, I'm an optimistic. Good grief, we muddled through 5 millennia of recorded history and I guess we came pretty close to incinerating it in 1962. But obviously the 20th Century has been a terrible experience because people didn't understand the ferocious technology that was out there and available to reek havoc on people. But World War I and World War II certainly proved that. And at least, since then, there hasn't been the types of mass holocaust that went on then.

PSD: Fred, what do you do to get away from it all and clear your head?

FS: I play tennis two or three times a week. I ski. I like to read as I mentioned a little while ago. I'm a sport fan. I love to watch football. I love to watch my kids play sports. So I have plenty of diversions other than just work. I like to work on business problems sometimes at home and sometimes on the weekend, but I'm not a workaholic. I don't sit and brew about FedEx all day long and I'm not sitting in my home sending and receiving emails. I think that the CEO has to set forth a vision. He or she has to get very good people, have them to buy in on that vision. They have to give them a lot of authority. They have to correct the strategy as it goes forward. But I don't think that it's something that requires every waking minute. And if you do, you won't make good decisions and you can't be contemplating.

PSD: You've been around the world and you've seen the amount of poverty.

FS: The amount of poverty and I believe we're a very big part, maybe the biggest part, of the solution to end that. The only way in the world that poverty around the planet can be stopped is for people to participate in the modern economic system. It's not a zero sum game. You don't have to have one winner and one loser. So many places around the world, I mean, they'll never be able to dig themselves out of the grinding poverty that they find themselves in unless they can become part of the modern trading world. And we're the links that allow them to do that.

PSD: There's really not a resource problem on this earth.

FS: No.

PSD: It's really a distribution problem.

FS: Absolutely. That is exactly right. I mean it's down

to the level of food. There's no food problem in the world, it's the distribution problem. Put a different way, a wealth problem. They don't have enough wealth in order to be able to pay for the distribution and get the kind of things they need to be able to be nourished and healthy.

PSD: So would you rather be remembered more as a human being than as the founder of FedEx?

FS: I mean, I don't think over that horizon. I don't sit and think, gee, I hope people will remember me as blank whatever it is. Whatever they do, that's fine. I mean, I'm not doing anything for prosperity. I'm just doing it because this is what I ought to be doing and how that comes out, that's the way I'm happy with it.

PSD: How do you get the most out of every day? Do you give thanks? Are you spiritual in that you think, wow, what a gift! Another day of life!

FS: Well, I'm not; I don't think I'm that contemplative. But I sometimes, during the day, compare all of the benefits and the pleasantries that I enjoy against the alternatives that so many people past and present have not and do not enjoy.

PSD: Do you ever think in terms of your own mortality?

FS: Listen, there's somebody here who spent two years in Vietnam. I think a lot about my own mortality, and I don't have any ambitions to leave any sort of legacy of any sort or at least not one that I shape. Whatever I am and whatever I did will speak for itself and that will be that. I will say this much, going back to your thing about relationships and what have you, whether it's marriage or anything else. The one secret of it, seems to me, is that you've got to be willing to go at least 50% of the way or 51% of the way. And if anybody in a relationship will take that view, or 75% or 80% then you would have a successful relationship. But if you're always expecting to be on the receiving end, you'll never have one. And it may be the case why people's goals and life views and what have you don't work. But to have any chance of success in any kind of relationship, business, personal or what have you, you've got to be willing to give more than you are getting. Then you'll be successful. That's my philosophy.

PSD: It's one of the golden rules in a sense.

FS: It is. You read the FedEx Manager's Guide, which I wrote. It's been much modified, but you will see in there a section which I put in 20 some odd years ago for our Manager's Guide that's taught in the FedEx Leadership School. Basically every single major religion in the world has exactly the same "golden rule." Every single religion, Hinduism, Buddhism, Christianity, Zionism, it's all the same. Every one of them has a quote along these lines. Basically, do unto others. It's in there because it works.

Henry Foster

"What I appreciate more than anything is life. Life is a very precious gift, which should be used in a constructive and positive way. I really believe that when all the scripts are written, you won't be measured by what you got in life, but by what you gave."

Senior Advisor to President Clinton on Teen Pregnancy Issues.

Backstory: I became aware of Dr. Foster when he was nominated for the post of Surgeon General and then later around his good work in the Nashville community. His intellect was so sharp and his laugh would burst forth often, filling the room with joy. After our initial interview, we shared several lunches and coffees where he would school me on multiple topics. Through his sharing and experiences I learned of the systemic nature of racism and white privilege. He was generous with me and patient, a born teacher, and a kind man.

PSD: You have had quite an interesting time of things lately, especially with the President and all of the national politics unfolding around you.

HF: Yes, really interesting. Let me tell you a story. When I had been nominated for Surgeon General, I was sitting in one of the rooms of the White House reading a book. And you know how sometimes you can be so engrossed in a book? Well, I didn't notice that someone was standing over me. It was the President. He said, "If you don't mind, what are you reading?" I said, "*Sleep Walking Through History* by Haynes Johnson." When we got up to the Oval Office, I saw that he had a lot of books that we both had read. He gave me this marvelous book called *The Gettysburg Address* by Gary Wills.

This is truly a marvelous little book. First of all, the Gettysburg Address was preceded by a speech that lasted three hours. The Gettysburg Address itself is only 272 words long and is the more profound speech.

The point I wanted to make, though, is that after that speech, this country was referred to as 'The' United States. Prior, it had always been 'These' United States. It changed us from a fragment to a oneness.

PSD: Lincoln was a magical human being. Is he one of your heroes?

HF: Oh yes, absolutely. You know why he is one of my heroes? Because he reminds me in many ways of my own approach to solving problems. I recognized very early in life that having the right answer or knowing the right thing is only part of the puzzle. The real challenge is how you implement the answer, how you make it work. It is great to have the right idea for world peace, but if you can't make it happen, what good is it? I have learned this through the years, but it is very difficult for some people because they see it as a compromise. You have to be able to balance idealism with pragmatism to reach a goal. Lincoln did so adroitly, balancing the factions around the issue of slavery. He kept walking the line to keep the country together.

PSD: Growing up were you influenced to be this type of problem-solver and thinker, or was it more of an innate thing?

HF: Sometimes you are a certain way and you really don't know why or how it happened. I think a part of it is in my DNA, my intrinsic make-up. But another part of it is in my own family's make-up. I grew up in the segregated south, in Pine Bluff, Arkansas, and I watched how my people negotiated the system. I think the most important thing, if you are looking for the great anchor, was that my folks had the greatest faith in the essence of the American way. My father used to tell us that freedom and justice were locked in the American Constitution. The key, he said, was education.

PSD: There must have been some thick, hard walls for you to penetrate and some sharp wire to crawl over.

HF: I think something else happened which I have a knack for. I find commonalities as opposed to differences. I don't care who the people are or what groups they belong to, but people basically have a lot more in common than they do differences. I have always been an optimistic, open person.

I have faith.

You get prepared by doing things. I went to the University of Arkansas and was the only African-American in a class of deep southerners. I was also the youngest person in the class, so I negotiated those four years, just like I had watched so many others do.

PSD: What led you into medicine?

HF: A few things come to mind. First, my father graduated from Morehouse College in 1928. That's the same college I graduated from in 1954. The family story was that my father was a pre-med student at Howard University in Washington, but didn't have the money to continue. This was during the height of the depression. So he took a job in Arkansas as a science teacher at a local high school to help support his family, because my mother was pregnant with my older sister. In a vicarious sort of way, going into medicine was fulfilling one of my father's desires.

Second, one of my father's best friends in life was Dr. Clyde A. Lawlah. We had an avuncular relationship. He was a black man who finished the University of

Chicago Medical School in 1932. I used to follow him around and carry his bag.

There is a third, more pragmatic factor. Opportunities were extremely rare for African-Americans in that genre. I knew this was a good way to help people. I liked medicine and had a pretty good aptitude for it.

PSD: Is it not what you do in the end but the process that matters?

HF: Indeed. I think, too, that somehow, I have never reached a point where I feel I have done enough. I am always looking for something else to do and I think that makes a difference. Some people are never completely satisfied with what they accomplish.

PSD: You get juiced on the process and what happens while it all unfolds.

HF: Absolutely. And I enjoy challenges.

When things fail, I pick up the pieces and try another approach. What I appreciate more than anything is life. Life is a very precious gift, which should be used in a constructive and positive way. I really believe that when all the scripts are written, you won't be measured by what you got in life, but by what you gave. I really believe that!

PSD: I have found this to be the case with many of the people I have been interviewing.

HF: There is another aspect to giving.

There are two kinds of broad definitions of wealth. One is occidental, and the other is oriental. Basically, the occidental definition of wealth is the acquisition and accumulation of possessions. But the oriental definition is having few needs. If you have few needs, I think it's true that you are wealthy. Because if you have all the money in the world but are unhappy and unfulfilled, then you are really quite poor.

PSD: If you are Taoist in nature, just sitting by a stream in bliss, then you are quite rich.

HF: Absolutely. That is what it is all about.

I have always been pleased with the things I have given. I am writing a book, by the way, which I think you would enjoy reading. I may call it Promises To Keep. The book is written around three themes: my early life, my healthcare years, and the nomination process.

I want to write a second book about how to intervene in the lives of inner city kids in a positive way.

PSD: You don't strike me as retaining any bitterness about what happened during the nomination process.

HF: The main reason I didn't get bitter was because I was pretty observant. A few hours after I was nominated, there were all kinds of people coming out to take stands opposing me. These people knew nothing about me. In fact, I could have walked into their offices and they would have had no idea who I was. So I realized very quickly that it was not about me, Henry Foster. That is why I came through personally unscathed. The hearings were my forum to address these accusers and reassure those who supported me. I wanted to also show my kids — because I have a future with them — that when a battle comes, you have to put up the best fight you can.

PSD: I was very pleased to see my friend Senator Bill Frist throw (through) his support behind you.

HF: I was, too. He backed me based on my

qualifications. One thing that was most disappointing was that I looked upon a Senate Committee as seeking truth. But the people who were on that committee who opposed me were not interested in truth. Had they known the truth and knew nobody else knew about it, they would have suppressed it. I guess I was a little naive.

PSD: That's scary, isn't it?

HF: Yes, and that's why it was so disappointing. They were not interested in the truth. We even had a sworn affidavit from the State of Alabama and from the patient that I was nowhere near the meeting in question. I was operating on a woman. The committee wanted to ignore the facts and still try to place me at this meeting.

PSD: That's sad. If they were just grilling you to make sure you were worthy of the position, you could have respected that.

HF: Of course I could. But once they had the truth and still chose to ignore it, that was disappointing. That is how politics has gotten. The real downside is that it's getting harder and harder to find people willing to subject themselves to that kind of scrutiny.

PSD: This was a good test of your positive philosophy. Not to trivialize it in any way, but for you, this was just a minor setback.

HF: You're right, especially from a personal standpoint. In January, 1996, President Clinton appointed me his Senior Advisor on teen pregnancy reduction issues. So I am doing a lot of things. Life goes on. I have two wonderful, independent adult children who are out there being good citizens, so life goes on.

PSD: What is Bill Clinton like as a person?

HF: Great. I really love him. He's such a neat person. I mean look at his background. His father was killed in a car accident when his mother was two months pregnant with him, so he never even knew his father. His mother worked in fill-in jobs and she was, as a woman, paid less. He's obviously very bright. You don't lead your law class at Georgetown University and become a Rhodes Scholar by being an idiot.

PSD: Are you a political person?

HF: Actually, most people assume I'm a Democrat but I'm actually independent. Though I supported Lamar Alexander for two terms. He was a good governor.

PSD: Can you share your philosophy in terms of raising your own children?

HF: To let them know that, no matter what they think, the best friends they will ever have in this world are their mother and father. Second, I have never pretended to have all the answers. I tried to make them aware of my foibles. Third, I had to make them aware of how the system worked. I had to be the one who was responsible for making the mistakes. I guess a lot of it is luck. I have seen friends of ours, who are good people, have kids that seemed absolutely possessed. We never even got a call for one of our kids throwing a spitball. Remember, kids pay a lot more attention to what you do than to what you say.

PSD: Based on your varied experiences, what advice would you give a young person?

HF: Realize how important it is to give of your talents. This is what I heard growing up from my family — "When you pass away from this place and your slate is written, you want it to be said that you did something to leave this world a better place than you found it." This is a fundamental philosophy. Everybody who has difficulty basically seeks relief. I am here to try to provide relief where and when I can to those who need it. And I try to seek relief when I need it.

PSD: So seek first to give rather than to receive?

HF: Think about it. When you really enjoy giving, as opposed to getting, you control your own fate and happiness. If I can be happy by providing for you then I'm in control. But if I have to wait to get something from you, then I'm at your mercy. This is true. When I was dealing with those poor, rural women in Alabama, nothing made me feel better than to put a smile on one of those faces. Nothing! Or a thank-you for being kind. To give these people a little respect just by referring to them as Miss Williams instead of Lucy.

PSD: You love people, I can feel it. Is that another innate quality?

HF: Yes, and it, too, is part of my upbringing. I grew up in an enclave so I was protected from a lot of the harshness of segregated American society. It never crossed my mind that anybody was better than somebody else just because of their birthright. I didn't think it worked like that. I figured God gave people different talents, and I was fortunate that God gave me a particular talent.

PSD: Will you share your views on the current state of race relations in America?

HF: Some things are better and some things are worse. It depends on what you focus on. I like to look at what's getting better. Sure, there's a bigger gap between certain classes because of what happened in the Reagan years. But what's happening to children in this country is unconscionable in terms of the amount of poverty. Six million children under 5 years of age live in poverty — here in the greatest of any industrialized nation in the world. Those things are all bad.

PSD: Why do we as a people allow such a thing?

HF: Because we are insensitive and uncaring. There are two reasons why it happens.

PSD: The blind devotion to the cult of materialism?

HF: Greed and avarice is a major part of it.

It's unconscionable that this nation, the wealthiest nation in the history of mankind, does not provide universal healthcare access to pregnant women and babies — the most vulnerable amongst us. It's not like the country is trying to tackle the problem of what to do with some 35 million people that are unemployed at any given time. That would be a monstrous task. Do you know how easy it would be to provide care for mothers and babies? It would be virtually nothing. There are only 4 million births in this country each year, and of that number, only 22% have inadequate access. We are talking about 880,000 people. We can provide superlative care for that whole cadre of women for the cost of two stealth bombers. The cost of one of those planes is 750 million dollars, and that does not include research and development.

PSD: The real tragedy is that we don't even need any of those planes.

HF: I know. We already have over 20 of them and to think that we could take about two-and-a-half of those bombers and provide all of that care. This is the biggest investment we can make in this country, assuring the quality of human reproduction.

PSD: Yet there's so much indifference in the world to what matters most.

HF: Indifference! Absolutely! I read that during World War II, pregnant women were given double rations in England. Not only did that not occur in this country, I doubt if anyone even thought about it. Our society has tended to punish women and pregnancy for the reasons of dollars and business.

PSD: Why don't we provide the services you advocate?

HF: I don't know. The bigger problem in this country right now is that we are getting government by default. Did you know that only 39% of Americans voted in 1992, and in 1994, only 37% — barely one in three? That boggles my mind. When I think about how this country was founded, your ancestors had come to escape serfdom and persecution, where you couldn't rise above your father's position at all. They came over here and built the greatest kind of democracy, have the franchise, and then fail to exercise it. To me, it is the weirdest thing how people fail to vote in this country. I think 80% of the people vote in Israel.

PSD: So the real enemy is apathy?

HF: Yes, that's right.

PSD: What can we do?

HF: There are a lot of things we have to do. We have to increase sensitivity. We have to put people in office who are more sensitive. We have to realize the value of investment. The author of Megatrends, John Naisbett, devoted a whole chapter showing the advantages of the long term over the short term. He also talked about how this country got so far behind by not planning ahead and investing in the future. Basically, when you take care of mothers and babies, what you are doing is investing in the quality and future of the country. But the country only looks at the cost of what it would take to care for these women. Maybe it costs two billion dollars. That is still only two of those airplanes.

PSD: Ours is, sadly, a very profit-oriented culture even at the expense of humanity.

HF: Right. I remember during the Nixon administration a phrase coming up that I just loved. It talked about the Republicans back then as 'people who know the price of everything and the value of nothing.'

PSD: But the babies you are talking about, they are the future of this country.

HF: Which reminds me of another point, that the greatness of this country has always come through its diversity. We need to make sure to maximize this diversity. Chuck Yeager, who grew up very poor, said he could have never done the things he had accomplished if he hadn't had access to such an excellent education. What happens when we see an elitist type of government forming is that we start squandering our most precious resource - brainpower. And it's something you cannot buy.

PSD: This needs to be addressed on a national level.

HF: What this country really needs is a domestic Marshall Plan. The best schools, the best day care, should be in the inner cities, or in Appalachia, where the needs are greatest. That is where the teacher/pupil ratio should be the highest — not the way it is now.

PSD: Do you see that happening?

HF: Well, that goes back to my previous thoughts about voting. It depends on what kind of people we choose to lead us. If we sit around and don't vote, what chance do we have? Churchill said, "Democracy is absolutely the worst form of government that has ever been created. Except for all the others."

PSD: Funny.

HF: But he is so right. You see the magic when the people who created this democracy were sitting around the Acropolis thousands of years ago. They did so at a time when you really had to sit around and think. There were no IRS forms to fill out, no TV. The magic is lost when you stay at home. We need to do a better job of teaching civics and responsibility. We did this with the civil rights movement in the '60s. I think schools should be turned out on Election Day and all the kids should be allowed to go the polls with their parents.

PSD: How much responsibility does the media have because of the tremendous amount of influence it possesses?

HF: There is certainly no codified responsibility, though there is a moral, human one to help these kids understand that their actions may lead to their deaths, like with AIDS. Where the paradox occurs is when those of us in this so-called free, open society want to teach our children about human sexuality and how to protect themselves, the conservative element rises up and says, "No, education is dangerous. It will make kids become more sexually active." How foolish can you be? All you have to do is turn on the TV and you'll see all kinds of behavior there. How can teaching them about the danger of HIV or AIDS hurt these kids?

What validates what I am saying is that in every industrialized nation where the pregnancy rates are 10% to 50% as high as ours, everyone has complete family life education in grades one through twelve. Teachers are not harassed or brow-beaten. We have to change all this.

PSD: How would you like to be remembered?

HF: Most importantly, as someone who tried to make the world a better place. Someone who was creative and had ideas, who had hope and who had faith. Someone who operated on four major principles; I tried to engage every task using intelligence, energy and enthusiasm, integrity, and persistence. That is how I try to approach problems.

PSD: Are you a spiritual man?

HF: Yes, I am very spiritual. I am proudly spiritual. We are all spiritual beings. We all have spirits. There is definitely a soul.

Eddie George
(New 20th Anniversary Content)

Eddie George was a running back in the National Football League for nine seasons. He played college football for Ohio State University and won the Heisman Trophy in 1995. George earned an MBA from Northwestern University's Kellogg School of Management. In 2016, he appeared on Broadway in the play Chicago as the hustling lawyer, Billy Flynn.

Backstory: Eddie and I had a cool karma in that we would run into each other all the time in unusual places, once even in South Beach, Miami. This was a bit strange because we didn't even know each other. One day I was talking about him at a small market and he literally walked in. He saw me and shook his head, "Brother, I swear to you I was just thinking about you." My lunch companion informed Eddie that I was talking about him as he walked in. He sat down with us and we all talked about the mystery that surrounds all of life.

Before leaving, I mentioned to Eddie that I was trying to get an interview with him for this book through the football team but was having no luck. He just smiled and said, "Come by the practice camp tomorrow in the afternoon, and we'll just do it."

So I did, and we did the whole thing in the locker room. In the years since then, I have come to admire Mr. George and his never-ending quest for personal growth and a deeper experience of being human.

PSD: You were born with a lot of ability. But how hard does a professional athlete work?

EG: I guess you work as hard as you want to work. You have individuals who are just naturally gifted and they can just go out there on Sundays and do it. But me personally, I like to feel as though I'm taking my game to another level. I don't want to see myself as the same as the year before. I want to be different, much improved, more skillful, a much more knowledgeable player than I was the previous year.

PSD: Were you always into self-improvement or did you kind of grow into it?

EG: I think I was pretty much into it. It took some time to develop. It took some time for me to see and to realize what the formula was for me to reach my goals. And that's always been my foundation.

PSD: Can you share your formula for improvement?

EG: My formula basically is to just keep working hard and never lose that edge, never lose that edge, never get complacent because once you reach a certain level you can become complacent which is fine. I like to give it my best every single time I go out on the field and find the peace within.

PSD: On top of professional athletics, you are also a father. Do you take that same philosophy to other areas of your life?

EG: That's been the key now. I'm learning to really grow as a man and make better decisions in the business field and take that philosophy that I've learned through the years playing football out into other areas of my life. Dealing with family, dealing with business, dealing with my son, and it's really working out for me.

PSD: So much is thrust upon a young athlete. And really when you think about it, you guys are only in your early 20's. Society, for the most part, does not demand a lot of the average individual at that age. How do you cope with the pressure?

EG: This is the downside. You can look at all the negative aspects of being in this situation. But you know, every situation has its pros and cons. It's all according to how you deal with it and how you handle it. It only becomes pressure if you allow it to be pressure.

PSD: Where do you find your inner strength?

EG: I more or less rely in the ability of God. I try to remain spiritual. I can't say that I'm some overly religious person, but I do I try to do spiritual well. I dig deep and draw back on my past experiences, what I've been through before, and go from my inner strength and my instincts to trust in myself, and basically that's what it's all about. I think I no longer look at problems as problems, even serious or major problems. I look at it as a situation that has to be handled.

PSD: It's beautiful that you mention God, because a lot of times people seem afraid to use the "God" word. God doesn't have to be linked to a particular religion or dogma. Were you always a spiritual person?

EG: No. I don't think you can be drilled into God. I think it comes through a person over time and how it's presented to them and it's their own experience. You can go to church every single day, or write out checks for poverty and give back to the community all you want in the name of God but not know God. Knowing God is in your heart and you feel it. And it's waking every morning and doing the best for your family and it's real. God's authentic and nothing you can touch. God is nothing made up. It's real.

PSD: Amidst the crazy and chaotic nature of your life, do you take quiet time to connect with this Source?

EG: It's throughout the day. It's just all throughout the day. It's good to pray and it's good to meditate within yourself, but it's all the time. Even speaking now, it's all the time.

PSD: Do you have a philosophy that the 'presence' we are talking about is in everybody and everything?

EG: I believe so. I think everything in this universe is definitely connected. And it's up to the eye, the eye that's unseen, that which you can't see, to realize that and to see the truth that's there. That's what I believe.

PSD: I would agree. Someone once said that the greatest things in the universe are never seen by the naked eye.

EG: Exactly.

PSD: I hear you saying that God is something more to be experienced than to be known with the intellect.

EG: Precisely.

PSD: Is that not the challenge for all of us whether you're an accountant or a football star?

EG: It's all connected and that's when success comes in. When you understand that, in any situation that you're in, whether it seems to be negative or positive, it's having a peace within and you can never go wrong. So when something goes wrong and it knocks you down and you deal with it. When something is actually overwhelming you with joy and excitement and it's positive, you're not really excited. It's having that balance. And that's what I really focus on—having a balance and being happy at my lowest point.

PSD: Not that one doesn't want to win, but in the scheme of a lifetime, or even a career, a bad play or even a bad game doesn't really amount to much.

EG: It puts it in perspective. It definitely puts it in perspective.

PSD: You sound like you define success from the

inside.

EG: Exactly. Like I said, I could win 7 billion titles, rush for 2000 yards, 7 years straight and be an All-Pro, and still not be happy. I think just being happy with myself and finding that inner peace within me—that definitely defines success for me. Also, being able to handle any situation at any given time, that's success to me. Knowing where my blessings came from and understanding, not just knowing, but understanding, and feeling it on a day-to-day basis, that's success to me.

PSD: This is an open-ended paradigm that is ever-evolving.

EG: Yes, never-ending.

PSD: It's a process, not a destination.

EG: Right. Because what happens when my career is over, which is a definite outcome? It's going to happen, and what if I say I'm not going to be happy until I've reached these goals? That's ridiculous because what if I never reach these goals? Over a period of time I learned that I needed to be happy with what I have now and where I am and where I'm headed, instead of saying, 'Oh man, I need to get better' and really pushing and being hard on myself. I just need to be happy and be thankful for what I have now because I may not ever go to that other level. And who's to say I will be even happier? Because you're going to want more and more and more. So I'm just more or less taking it as it comes and just enjoying life.

PSD: Like a mirage, once you arrive at the illusion, it is not the same thing you were approaching with such high expectations.

EG: Well said. And yes, once you get it, it's not the same.

PSD: Because you feel so blessed, is there a sense of wanting to give something back to the greater whole?

EG: I tell you I like to give back even if it is as we're talking now...

PSD: An interview?

EG: An interview or talking to a kid that wants to listen and wants to learn. I deal with my son on a daily basis and talk a lot to my mother. You want to set up organizations, but I don't want to deal with the publicity, just so someone might say, "Hey, he's a great guy." You know, I want to do it because I mean it and it comes from the heart.

PSD: Rather than a publicity stunt, your approach sounds much more...

EG: Inspired.

PSD: Yes!

EG: It's not like, 'Okay, you all just set this up and I'll just come and make an appearance every two days and (just) make me look good.' I mean, that's cool for whatever you want to do for your image and how you want people to perceive you, but I don't care about that. Because you always know you're not going to please everybody, so you might as well do what's in your heart.

PSD: You sound like you know who you are, or at the least discovering yourself.

EG: Yes, I'm learning. It takes some time. You know, I think I'm still learning who I am.

PSD: Because the 25-year-old Eddie George is not

going to be the same as the 35-year-old Eddie George.

EG: Exactly.

PSD: If I asked in this moment, "Who are you?" what would you say?

EG: Right now I'm a man that was a boy. I was a boy growing into a man and I'm realizing a lot of different things in my life. Reality has definitely hit me in between the eyes, and I'm learning to accept a lot of things. I think I'm evolving into a greater man than I was a year ago or two years ago.

PSD: That's beautiful. Did your mom raise you primarily?

EG: My mother and my grandmother.

PSD: You came from a strong maternal background. Is it a challenge for you to be a father growing up without a strong male role model?

EG: Yes. It's very challenging to be a father. Especially when you have a son and he looks up to you. It's so funny. Just the other day, I was with my son and he more or less wants to do everything that I do, like with the car keys, he wants my car keys. So I gave him another set. But he doesn't want them. He wants my car keys, my hat, my phone because he's emulating me. So I have to make sure that I do the right thing so he can see, not to just go in my footsteps per se, but kind of have an idea which route he wants to take.

PSD: What would you tell your son if he were 18 and about to go to Europe with a backpack?

EG: Enjoy it over there. It's beautiful and be careful. Be careful what you come across. Just protect yourself in all aspects and enjoy it. Get to know yourself. Find yourself and then tell me about it. I mean, I really enjoy hearing about how people travel and when they experience different things, going to different scenes. Whatever he wants to do, he has my ultimate support.

PSD: Being there for him as he finds himself?

EG: Exactly. Because we're all put on this earth for a reason. I'm pretty sure that I'm not going to put pressure on him to be athletic, or a doctor, or a lawyer. Find yourself and you define yourself. And I'll just guide you and tell you whether I think it's right or wrong. I believe that at 18, 19, or 20 you should be becoming a young adult and he needs to hear certain things for himself to decipher from each experience, different things to know what I'm talking about. Hey, you're going to fall in life, so he's going to have to go out there and I have to let him go.

PSD: Drugs, guns in schools, AIDS...Among many things, what would you tell the young people that face these challenges today?

EG: What would work for me?

PSD: Yes. What works for you.

EG: I guess, in a round about way, I was in that same situation. There was a point in my early career, my early life in my adolescence, when I was unstable. But I've always had it in the back of my mind that I was going the make it in this profession. I was going to get there, someway somehow. I didn't know how it went, but I was going to get there. It's always been in the back of my mind and as the years went on, it became a passion for me to work out and find different ways to get better. Then I saw myself getting better and I'd say, "Man, this is addicting, I want to do it more. I want to do it more, I want to be the best I can be."

PSD: So a person has to find what they love, whatever it is, and put their passion behind it?

EG: Whatever it is, whether it's music, whether it's writing, whether it's speaking, whether it's being a doctor or a garbage man. It's the passion, it's that love. I mean, it's that love that shows in your work. You know, it's not a mechanical thing. It comes from within and is flowing.

PSD: So find what you love and do it for yourself?

EG: Yes, for yourself, for your family, for God…

PSD: Please talk about your mom. Are the two of you very close?

EG: Well, Mom and I, we understand right now where I've decided to do my own thing and be my own man. And she's "You're my baby" and she's protecting me. She's very good. She's a great listener and I do listen to her and I guess our relationship has been more like brother and sister over the past years rather than like mom and son.

PSD: Maybe it's hard for her to let go?

EG: Yes. I mean, I'm her only son. I can kind of put myself in her shoes and understand where she's coming from. So just to ease her mind, I have to do things and show her that hey, it's okay, I'll be all right. Just be there and support me. I'm going to fall and make mistakes, but just be there.

PSD: You're doing what you love. Do you wake up some mornings and just think, "Man, this is amazing. This is great!"

EG: It's a rush, man! You sit back sometimes—I sit back at my house or I'm driving somewhere—and it's that feeling that everything seems right, like you're in another zone. You know, the day is nice, the sun is out, the windows are down, the music is on and everything is just, (Pauses) you feel good about everything. And that's what I'm like now. You know, I'm very fortunate because I'm healthy and everything is going so well.

PSD: You're healthy, famous, successful, and rich! Things could be much worse (Laughs).

EG: I know. I need to take advantage of this now. I need to enjoy myself.

PSD: What would you tell the kid with the Eddie George poster on his wall who someday wants to take a few snaps in the NFL?

EG: Brother, just stay focused. I mean, it's an old cliché, but it definitely works and you really have to stay focused. You can't just think about it. You have to stay focused, I mean it's everyday decisions. What are you going to do? It's a Friday and your friends want to go out. For instance, doing all the extra stuff. That's what I mean by staying focused. It's making a decision for what you want to do. You can always say, "Well, you know I'll put it off until tomorrow." But tomorrow never comes. It never comes. So I've always personally tried to separate the two. Like when I know that my competition is out partying or doing other things, I'm making a conscious effort to go and do a little something.

PSD: Have you always been so competitive?

EG: Oh yes. I hate to lose. And I try to not show it sometimes, but I really hate to lose.

PSD: Talk about what it's like to be somebody who grew up with very modest means and then, all of a sudden, look in your checkbook and see this great affluence.

EG: I just deal with it. I think it's great that I can go out and be able to afford certain things and not really have to worry about it. But by the same token, I have to be consciously aware that maybe tomorrow I'm going to never play another down. Could I live the same way the next 30 years and beyond? And could my son be okay as far as his education and his future?

PSD: Are you surprised how the modern athlete is held in such hero status these days?

EG: Well, you're seen as almost gods. Because, if you look at Jordan, who I admire, he's the ultimate. It was not his athletic abilities so much. But it was his drive and his whole story that I admire tremendously. He was not only a great athlete, but he went beyond that great athletic status and took it to another level, which was spiritual. Because he looked within himself and he found a deep, inner strength. He was real modest and humble about it and he just had the drive.

PSD: Beyond football, do you have dreams?

EG: Oh yes, definitely. Right now I'm trying to establish a business state of mind and keep the competitive edge in that. Right now I don't have a definite plan on what I want to do, but I'm opening up the doors for it.

PSD: How much did having a child change you?

EG: It's continual change.

PSD: Life without sleep.

EG: (Laughs) It has definitely changed me a lot. Seeing another little me in my arms and as he grows and I grow. When I see him, he's talking and able to hold conversations, and he has some sense of understanding now, it's amazing. It's absolutely amazing.

PSD: How would you like to be remembered as a human being?

EG: That's a heavy question.

PSD: Perhaps heavy, yet surely inevitable.

EG: It's inevitable. I mean I want to be remembered as a man that loved what he did and was really passionate. He was a warrior, that he was genuine and had a very great heart. I mean, I don't want a whole list of accolades and everything that I've accomplished. I just want to be known as a man that was loving and caring and did the best he could do for his family.

PSD: Any thoughts on that magical word love?

EG: Love can't be seen. It's just more or less felt. You can sense someone who truly cares about you or loves you. I really know I love my son.

PSD: Perhaps love is the great unseen.

EG: Yes, I believe so.

Bonnie Johnson, RN

"What I would say is that the God force or Great Spirit is greater than our skepticism. It is not limited by us. The idea that we have to have faith in order for spirit to work in this world is ludicrous to me. It is egotistical."

Holistic Healer

Backstory: Outside of my parents, Bonnie has had the greatest impact on my life. When the world broke my heart with its brutality and unconscious way, God sent me an angel to put it back together in the form of this humble healer. I could write a whole series about my experiences with Bonnie, and in fact I describe some of them in great detail in my book, *Martha's Vineyard Miracles*. She is my spiritual Godmother and mentor.

I knew when I started this book 20 years ago that I had to have Bonnie participate. Of course she declined, since she did not want to call attention to herself. But after I wouldn't stop begging and pointed out how many people would hear about Healing Touch, she finally relented. God bless her and the love she manifests in the world.

PSD: How did you get involved with holistic healing?

BJ: Going way back in my life, you'd see that what I have always been doing, in one way or another, is caring for people — even as a small child. I have always been a caregiver for children. I loved kids. So what I got interested in was finding some way in which I would be interacting with and caring for children. That's what led me to nursing, where I experienced the fullness in caring for children. At the same time, I was aware that there was so much that we weren't doing for people.

PSD: The nursing profession has gone through a lot of changes.

BJ: Yes, I am an old nurse, you see. I graduated from nursing school back in 1965, and have seen nursing go through all kinds of changes. A lot of those changes took us further and further away from contact with people and more and more into giving pills and operating machines. When I trained, I learned how to give a back rub to somebody in the morning, afternoon, and evening. That was just what you did. There are not many nurses who get trained to do that now, or who would even think about it. Not only are we working more and more with machines, but the patients are treated like machines, too. So I became very dissatisfied with that kind of treatment.

PSD: There must have been a sense of alienation that soon began to grow within.

BJ: I soon became aware that my view of people — my way of interacting — was not the same as other nurses. I thought, 'Am I the only one who wants to know patients on an individual basis, who believes that patients are in charge of their own healing?' The attitude that I saw a lot of was that the nurse, the doctor, and the health care facility knew what was best. To me, this wasn't right. I felt like I was in a desert, knowing that there was water out there somewhere. So I started searching for some way to bring more of what I knew instinctively and intuitively into the work I do with people.

PSD: So you made a break with traditional nursing practice?

BJ: It led to me going on what I call a spiritual journey twelve years ago. And it was an intentional spiritual journey. I decided to set aside a year without being actively involved in any social situations — I was just going to take care of my family. What a laugh! As if you only needed to take a year to do a spiritual journey. It actually took me a whole year just to find some books I could read and people to converse with about what I was looking for. I wasn't even sure what I was looking for! Some time into the second year, a very good friend I had gone to college with recommended a book to me, Therapeutic Touch. When I read it, I said 'This is it! This is what I want to do!'

PSD: So an inner light went on?

BJ: Yes. From that moment on, there was never any doubt that this was my life's work.

I just studied that book from the inside out. I talked to anybody and everybody who would listen to me about the phenomena of therapeutic touch. The process itself is very simple, so I read the book and did what it said to do. Then if someone said, "I have a headache," I would say 'Let me try this.' Of course, I had no real idea of what I was doing. I remember, at the time, I was working as a pediatric nurse at Vanderbilt. A good friend took me aside one day and said, "I am really worried about you and this stuff. I'm afraid the devil has got you!" And I thought, 'What is she talking about?' None of my experiences with this practice had been harmful in any way, so how could she say this? It was just a sincere question coming from a good friend.

PSD: A lot of people are afraid of metaphysical and holistic approaches, believing they might be satanic or evil. Is this a result of fear and ignorance?

BJ: There are a lot of people that have been taught there is only one way to live, and if you deviate from that one way, you will be in great harm. A force will take you over.

They believe that is true.

PSD: How many years have you been doing holistic healing?

BJ: Probably 9 or 10 years. I am still studying.

PSD: How would you best explain the process of therapeutic touch to someone who was unfamiliar with the experience?

BJ: It is very hard to put into words, but very easy to show. Most people have actually experienced it as children or even as adults when they were sick. Often times when people have fevers, one of the things others will do in caring for them is use their hands to brush the hair back from the forehead. This brushing motion is often therapeutic touch, because all the elements are there: a person who is in need, and a person who cares. The caring person brings her love, care, focus, and compassion — which is a basic element of therapeutic touch — to the one who is in need. All of this, along with the brushing, helps to restore order to the person and bring harmony. It is mystical and magical, and is unexplainable in terms of how something so simple could do so much.

PSD: Is the practice you have described similar to the laying on of hands in the biblical tradition?

BJ: Yes. One of the major differences is that both the healer and the person who is ill 'must believe' in order for the laying on of hands to work. This is not the case with therapeutic touch. One can actually be skeptical and still provide for the person's needs. Many therapeutic practitioners do have faith and strong belief, but it is not mandatory for the process to work.

What I would say is that the God force or Great Spirit is greater than our skepticism. It is not limited by us. The idea that we have to have faith in order for spirit to work in this world is ludicrous to me. It is egotistical.

PSD: How would you define success on a personal level?

BJ: Success is being fully who I am and really being true to that. Kind of staying in line with who I am and honoring it.

PSD: To thine own self be true.

BJ: I basically live a peaceful life. I was brought up in the tradition of a Protestant work ethic, and productively worked many years in that lifestyle. So I sometimes get caught up in the fact that there are a whole bunch of people out there that are very, very physically and/or emotionally ill. Since I have technical nursing skills, why am I not out there bandaging people, running machines, and throwing medicine at them on top of everything else I do? It's hard when I get challenged by that. So I tell myself, 'You have already done that for thirty years. They only ask for twenty in the army.' (Laughs)

PSD: It's not as if you are laying out back on the hammock.

BJ: Right. But what comes up is the fact that right now what I do is so easy for me, because this is my life's work.

PSD: We are sometimes culturally brainwashed to believe that it has to be difficult.

BJ: Yes. In the work I do, self-care is essential. So a lot of my day is self-care, in one form or another.

PSD: Can you talk about some of the things you do to help maintain self?

BJ: The kind of self-care that I do is to spend a lot of time with myself so I know who I am. One of the ways

I lose track of who I am is to be really, really busy. So I am a strong guardian of my time, because I've had years of experience of being busy, busy, busy.

PSD: So you give yourself the gift of completely unstructured time?

BJ: Yes. Just time where I am not with anybody else and I'm not doing anything else. I will spend time going for a walk, but usually do a walking meditation as part of it. Or I do Tai Chi, which is energy-moving. Creative movement is the new word for it. I read an article stressing exercise, suggesting that it sounds better to say, "I'm going to do my creative movement now." I also do a sitting-still meditation.

There's another recent practice called 'ceaseless praying'. I had gone for a walk, and while walking, was praying for procrastinators. The reason is that I had been in a conversation with my husband, and he said, "Well, pray for me, will you?" because he's a procrastinator. So I'm walking and praying for procrastinators. As I was just about to turn into my driveway, this little red Toyota caught my attention. A woman rolled down her window and said, "I'm looking for Bonnie Johnson. Do you know where she is around here?" And I said, 'Yes, I'm Bonnie Johnson.' She was just checking out where I was because somebody had given her my name. We got to talking and she said, "You know, I have this real problem with procrastination."

PSD: Synchronicity! So the key, for you, is to guard your time. That's where you have a weakness.

BJ: Yes. The part that's so hard for me is that I love being with people and doing things — something fun.

PSD: How would you suggest that people find a

deeper connection to themselves, so they can then be true to what they discover?

BJ: A lot of times, young people do not have enough consciousness or awareness.

So the journey to discovering who they are comes through stumbling. You get into all kinds of experiences without realizing that they're helping you know who you are. The most helpful way is through self-observation. How do you do that? How do you learn to observe anything? If you don't know how to observe yourself, start by observing other people, the environment. Watch what the cat is doing. Learn the skill, then go inward to observe yourself.

PSD: What do you feel is your biggest challenge right now?

BJ: Let me think. Do I have a challenge? It doesn't seem like the right word for me. I keep exploring the best ways for me to be present with the gifts I have, so I'm open to where that will be.

PSD: Is your life about service?

BJ: Yes. That's why I'm here. I have had many invitations to leave, but I turned them down. I'm here for the duration, to see it through. To be here with people, with this universe, in a way that can assist and help.

So I stay here to do that.

PSD: The challenge is to bring the core of who we are to wherever we go.

BJ: Yes. My son is in prison, so I visit the prison once a week. I spend three to six hours there. It's not an easy place to be. But I can choose to be present wherever I end up being.

PSD: Family usually presents us with unique challenges and learning.

BJ: Yes. My biggest challenge comes from seeing somebody in need, knowing I have the skills to be of assistance, yet they cannot receive. To watch someone in pain and suffering is so hard for me at times. I have to remember that the offer of healing is sufficient. When people can receive it, they will. My work is to keep on offering the healing and being there for them.

PSD: Do you ever get discouraged or feel overrun by the vast amount of suffering there is in this world of ours?

BJ: I get really angry about it and tend to rail at God. If we are supposed to be learning from all of this pain and suffering, then it's a screwed-up system. So I get angry. This usually happens when I have lost who I am. I'm out there pounding against a rock going nowhere. I have a really hard time with the suffering we inflict on each other. I question the whole idea that we or our souls have chosen to come here.

PSD: Who do you admire and why?

BJ: The people I admire most are the ones who are willing to put themselves and their wounds out there. By doing so, they are helping others and themselves heal.

PSD: What would you like your friends to say about you when that beautiful moment of passing finally comes and you move on to whatever you are to be?

BJ: I want people to wear bright colors, to dance and sing, to eat hot fudge sundaes, to enjoy that day. What I would like someone to say is "She was there when I needed her, and I could count on her. She was present."

Bobby Drinnon
(New 20th Anniversary Content)

Bobby Drinnon is a world-renowned intuitive and reader of the mystery.

Backstory: For years I heard people talk of a legendary psychic in East Tennessee, but I didn't know if he was a real man or simply a myth. One day I ran into a guy who spoke of Bobby and even had his office number. So I rang him up and, to my surprise, he invited to come spend a weekend at his farm. Bobby could not be a warmer, more gentle soul, and he had a fabulous sense of humor. For a while we kept in touch and he would let me know when he was coming to Nashville so we could share some time. One of my most interesting experiences with him occurred years later when we had fallen out of contact. I was sitting in Yankee Stadium in New York watching a baseball game, when all of a sudden I had the strongest feeling of Bobbie. I silently sent him a message of love and brotherhood. A few moments later my cell phone rang and it was him. "I got the message, brother, and I love you too."

PSD: When did you first realize that you had a gift?

BD: You mean a curse? (Laughs) I think when I was a child, about 4 years old, I started seeing things around me and was sensitive and then I started dreaming. The first dream I ever had that was intuitive was of me. I dreamt I was going to eat a bacon sandwich in a sandbox and this big kid was going to kick sand all over me and throw my bacon sandwich in the dirt. The next morning I got up and my mom was cooking a bacon sandwich. She hands it to me and tells me to go play. I go out to play and here comes this guy named Bobby Brewer. I still remember his name. And he looks at me and says, "You're some kind of 'person.'" And then he kicks sand all over me and throws my sandwich down. And I went berserk because I thought I was crazy.

PSD: That would be difficult.

BD: And it got so bad that I couldn't separate reality from dreams for a long time. It made me very nervous that I was crazy. Then I started seeing auras around people, haziness around people. And so it was at a young age that I knew something was really different.

PSD: How long did it take you to accept that your gift was a gift?

BD: I was starting to understand it at about 16 or 17. There was an old black lady named Mary Francis Whitaker. She's dead now, but she lived across the street from my grandmother in the town that I was born in and she was a witch. We called her a witch. She read coffee grounds and she really was a saint but people didn't understand then like they do today. And so she told me "You've got a gift, boy."

PSD: This is fascinating, please continue.

BD: I went back to her when I was 16. The first thing I ever did when I got my driver's license was I went back to her. I went on her porch and I sat down with her and said, "You said something to me when I was little boy." And she said, "I've been waiting for you for a long time." And she said, "You've got a gift and here's what your gift is." That was when I was 16 years old and it just evolved.

PSD: Can you describe what you do?

BD: I call myself an intuitive consultant because I do a lot of spiritual counseling. I think everybody has their own spiritual trip and turns out to be enlightened on their trip. I've dreamed about people the night before —now not everybody—but I do dream about a lot of people. So with the dreams I first get an impression and with the auras I try to put together a package that enlightens them and helps them. Plus some people come for specific reasons like a missing child or something like that. I want to really help people.

PSD: So it sounds like a partnership that you're working with somebody.

BD: Yes, it is a partnership and we work together. But I just have a story that all comes together.

PSD: Does everybody have some sense one way or the other of their own intuitiveness?

BD: Everybody has it. You can deny it. You can call it good or bad, but everybody's born with it.

PSD: What do you do to get yourself to become as open a channel as possible?

BD: I meditate a lot and I use meditation and dreams. There was a kid missing in Knox City up in upper East Tennessee, and his mother brought me a jacket of his. He was missing from a boat. I fell asleep on the bed with that jacket and I dreamt where he was. So I sent the divers down there and he came up out of the water like he was holding a basketball. He was that swollen.

PSD: How about in terms of finding one's destiny. Do you have any insight you could share?

BD: In terms of one's destiny, certain laws are set up that aren't changeable, and those laws are very predictable. I never thought it was predictable so you can tell people like if someone has diabetes and they're sad and they don't know it yet and you can say, "Take this kid to the doctor." Or if the child alone is going to be angry or is an adopted child who doesn't know their parents and you can say, "Okay, that adopted child has lung disease in their genes." And they would never have known that but then they can start treating them early.

PSD: How about with people's fears?

BD: Fear is a big reason people come to me.

PSD: I would assume because, if you weren't afraid of what was going to come your way, you would not have a strong desire to know the future.

BD: Yes. The beauty of what I've been able to do is what I wanted to do in the beginning, and that is helping people get in here. (He points to his heart.) That's what I want to do. Because if you give them the tools to get in here, then the future really doesn't matter very much.

PSD: Right. And also, not in any way to demean what anyone's future events are, but in a sense the circumstances would seem trivial compared to what goes on inside of us.

BD: Yes. But when most people think of enlightenment, they think this concerns who they're married to and what kind of car they drive. So the state of the future is important to them.

PSD: You're talking about their identity, right?

BD: Yes. I think the biggest suffering in people today comes because we've been taught by the media and everything else that this is the way life should be. So if they see their life and future not going the way it should, then they're miserable. That's why you have to teach people it didn't go the way it should because of the way it is. You bring them from that delusion or illusion into reality. Also, everybody who comes in the door has a different need and that's what I love about it.

PSD: How does one detach from drawing one's identity from external things and drawing it out from within ourselves?

BD: First, you have to teach people that. I mean, that's what I try to do everyday: just teach people that one concept. It can be life-changing.

PSD: We don't teach it in schools.

BD: No, and God bless religion. But a lot of religions teach you everything but that.

PSD: I don't see the media, which is advertisement-driven, teaching people to be independent.

BD: No. But people judge a lot based on what's on television. But you have to teach people they don't have to do that. Otherwise, they will have a vision of the future that is unrealistic. And then when they don't get it, they're miserable.

PSD: What would you tell a youngster right now, or any person who's reading this, if you were going to counsel them, to help them get in touch with themselves?

BD: The basic philosophy that I teach, and I live it everyday, is that we come from God. We are all seeds of one God. That's why I have never understood prejudice. When we're born, God puts two things in place within us: he puts inside of us a higher self and he puts inside of us a lower self. The lower self is selfish desire and anger and fear. The higher self is love and compassion and a connection with God. The trick of life is, you either choose to see things on an earth-bound level, so you're probably pretty angry and messed up in life, or you see it from the spiritual angle.

The lower-self choice is sin. That's what sin is to me. It's not choosing to see it from a higher self. Also, God weaves a weakness in each human being on purpose. I believe in trying to correct that weakness, whether it be fear or anger or violence, you come to God to cure your weakness.

PSD: Right. And you come to God from dwelling within?

BD: Yes.

PSD: It's not an external entity. God would be within and within each and every one of us, so there are no favorites.

BD: No, no favorites. And the beautiful part is why I love teaching people. Because this is the only thing in which we're different than animals. We can reinvent ourselves. So you teach people they're originally born this way. But what happens is most people come into the beauty of life and then they're automatically put into a box. And this box has five sides: society, parents, TV, media, and religion. Now sadly, most people die in this box. This is their whole world. And you have to teach people individually how to free themselves from religion, how to free themselves from society. And if you can get them out of the box, the next step is reaching a place where you never get too high or too low, never too far to the right or too far to the left. We want to teach people how to exist mentally here.

PSD: To exist in the center?

BD: You can be spiritual without being religious, but you can't be religious without being spiritual. I mean, the spirituality is the act of connecting with God from within you. So you teach people to get rid of their low esteem and guilt and fears. I want to write a book one day called "Religion Ran Me to the Bible." Because I'll tell you, I was taught so much fear that I had to go look for myself in the bible and see that God really does love Bobby Drinnon individually as a person. God lives in me.

PSD: With all of our perceived imperfections...

BD: Yes, of course. He lives in me and if he lives in me, for me to disrespect myself or allow you to disrespect me is a disrespect of God. But for me to disrespect you, it's the same equal thing. So we all see the God within each other. And we worship or not worship, but we see that seed in each other. If you can teach people how to get to this, come out of the box and make the right decision based on their higher self instead of their lower self, then you teach them to get here. There are three ways you can do that. You have to come to some agreements in your life of the laws of life.

PSD: Well, walk me out of the box first a little bit. Because most people in the box are saying, well, how do I get out of this box?

BD: Well, getting out of the box means you must come to terms with these things. You can use everything. You know, people talk about dysfunctional families. I've never seen a functional one.

PSD: Yeah, it's an oxymoron.

BD: (Laughs) It is an oxymoron. So you teach people that we came here in vehicles—bodies. So let's make peace with the vehicle and get a grip. Let's get over this.

PSD: Unless this function is to teach that lesson.

BD: Sure. Then you teach people, you know, school. 'Little Johnny's got to make good grades.' You must teach people to be your own self. Get away from society. I mean, this is not an easy thing. Because everybody's lesson is different. But you must not live for people. You cannot live for people. If there's one thing I would say to the world, it's you've got to live right with yourself. You've got to live right in your mind. You have to live in freedom. I don't care what it is. Even if you have to go to jail for your beliefs, live in freedom. Even if you have to die for your beliefs, live in freedom.

PSD: And teach the world by being an example…

BD: Yes. And you don't beat up on religion. I respect religion, but religion is a good car to get there. But it isn't going to get you where you need to be unless you do it. God won't move a parked car. You've got to get in and move the car. So you say to somebody, "Is it possible in your life that you were taught through religion maybe to fear God to such a point that you can't get to God? And as you teach them to see that God lives in them, then they get past this part of the box.

PSD: James Joyce said, "Religion is the defense against the religious experience."

BD: Yeah, it is, best defense. So then you teach people how they can't live their whole lives based on this TV and media thing. You know, you can't live your life based on the television. And you know, people do. They really do.

PSD: Which is, in effect, letting other people dictate to you who you are and should be.

BD: I don't want to go to dinner tonight with you and have such bad manners that I'm ignorant. I mean there's a difference. I don't want be a maniac with these things.

PSD: So you get out of the box by defining yourself

first?

BD: You've got to go in and see what the box did to you. And then you've got to strive to get out of it. So the next step is getting your mind to a place where you stay even. Three ways I did this in my life: I made acceptance of the laws of people. I mean, I made acceptance of the laws of life. I accepted the laws of people, and I learned to control my mind. Because I'm going to tell you, the laws of people state, the laws of life state that life and death and good and bad health and joy and suffering and good and bad events will happen to me and you forever. There's no way around it. It's the only thing that makes life fair. The Pope has to go through these laws. The President goes through these laws.

PSD: Right. The richest man in Tennessee two or three years ago died of cancer within 6 months. He couldn't do anything to buy an extra day.

BD: He can't do a thing about it. So we're all even under these laws. People say this is unfair. But I don't think so.

PSD: All of those things are based primarily on fear.

BD: On fear. But if I get up in the morning and I understand that if someone criticizes me to stay calm because someone is going to compliment me. If someone compliments me I'm not going to get too cocky because someone is going to insult me. It's a circle. I swear it is. So the next thing I do is learn to control my mind. Because the mind is like a monkey in a cage jumping around. If you don't control it, it's going to control you. So God gave you no choice in the laws of life. Zero. He gave you no choice in the laws of people. Zero. He did, however, rig your mind to where you can control how the laws affect you. That's the only thing you can do.

PSD: This space between stimulus and response.

BD: Correct.

PSD: Mental awareness, consciousness.

BD: It is awareness and consciousness. And we're going to die someday. And people are going to hate you someday and they're going to hate me someday. But those are the levels. These circles are never-ending change. So this is kind of what I try to believe in and teach and try to stay in tune with my higher self.

PSD: Love is the magic ingredient.

BD: It's it.

PSD: It can heal anything?

BD: It heals everything. Jesus was right and so was the Buddha.

PSD: They're all saying the same thing.

BD: They all say the same thing.

PSD: How do I be more compassionate?

BD: You have to use different stories. Like you take somebody and you say to a man, well, try to visualize, do an exercise in compassion. So try to sit with some stranger and look at them in intensive care dying, all plugged up to these machines, try to have compassion. But he may not even care about that. But you take his hunting dog and you say, "Try to see the hound dog caught in the trap," or something like that. And they can show compassion and hopefully transfer that into the love of people.

PSD: What advice would you give someone reading, in terms of becoming not only more intuitive but more aware?

BD: Well, I think getting a sense of yourself. You've got one trip, one shot, get it. Get who you are. You're perfect, you're okay. I don't care who you are, you're okay. No trip here is a waste and every day is a magical journey. I'll tell you why I don't get depressed. In 20 years, I've never been depressed and never been lonely. I do so because I have learned to live in a state of gratefulness. Gratefulness for the pain, gratefulness for the enemy, gratefulness for learning problems. I want to be in a state of gratefulness.

PSD: Yet in this universe of polarity, we will always have suffering.

BD: As long as you have insecurities and people killing each other over religion, you will have suffering. The only thing we can ever hope for is to enlighten people to the point where they can say, "I'm a religious person on a spiritual chair and I'm trying to get in touch with my spirituality," which involves Christians being understanding of Muslims and Muslims being understanding of Christians. I can't change the universe, but maybe I can change 8 people a day and 40 people in a week.

PSD: How do you define success for you personally?

BD: I already have everything I want. I want nothing else. I don't want any fame. I make enough money to be okay. I've been married and done it all, and I'm just happy sitting right here. Success to me is being able to do that. Also, success to me is simply being able to walk down the steps everyday.

PSD: So just to participate in God's great dream for a

few more breaths?

BD: Participating in God's plan for me, which I just wish I knew at 16 of course...because I could have been so much farther in this thing. But I don't want to be on television much. I don't want to be the 'fake of the week' and I don't want to market myself. I'm like you and the reason I'm doing this and I told you this is because I believe your spirit led you here. And I believe God will maybe touch someone through this and what you are doing.

PSD: If even one person reads it.

BD: Or can use it and is blessed, or can be blessed.

PSD: It's funny. When I wrote my first book, I realized near the end of editing it I thought, 'You know, if only one person reads this and is changed, the project is a success.' A moment later I had this profound realization that I already had accomplished this, because it had changed my life.

BD: Exactly. That's it.

PSD: What is your connection with the rainbow?

BD: When I was a little kid, I was scared of everything, because I was taught this by my mother. I mean, these people were scared of everything—even a chicken—anything and everything. Storms were my biggest fear. But when the rainbow came, I knew the storm was over. So it made me feel secure.

PSD: How would Bobby Drinnon like to be remembered for this one life?

BD: Kindness. Just kindness. I'm mischievous and I'm a kid. Just to say Bobby was kind to me. He smiled at me at the grocery store. You know, he bought me some food sometimes and was kind.

Ron Bombardi, Ph.D

"You must learn to think for yourself. No one else can do your thinking for you. You must have your own reflective life if you want to capitalize on this sense of a difference between being knowledgeable and being wise. Wisdom is the way you live, not the things you say."

Professor of Philosophy, Middle Tennessee State University

Backstory: For no other reason than to learn, I decided to take a few philosophy courses at MTSU. Through a stroke of luck I stumbled upon the greatest teacher I had ever experienced in an academic setting, Dr. Bombardi. He ran his classes like Socrates. We gathered in circles. He was a participant in the quest, more guide than guru, and he always challenged us to go deeper. I eagerly looked forward to his classes because I was never sure what our point of inquiry might be or what morsel of truth might be discovered. Ron was open and accessible and generously allowed me to sit in his office for hours in dialogue. A humble man, he initially refused to participate in the book, but I stayed on him and eventually he acquiesced.

PSD: Were you a philosophical kid?

RB: I was a pretty dorky kid, not very athletic, kind of egg-headed. While most kids spent their summers improving their physical skills, I was in a basement with my nose buried in a book. I read The Rise and Fall of the Third Reich when I was 11 years old. I had that sort of temperament, so I was very self-sustaining.

PSD: How did you become a teacher of philosophy?

RB: I thought I would always wind up, in one way or another, being a professional philosopher. I didn't always know that would mean the kind of commitment to undergraduate teaching, which sort of came my way. I was 16 or 17 years old when I realized I was really good at this.

When I was 17, I had a certain formative experience. I

was not a popular kid, I wasn't used to other kids seeking me out. I was usually running away from them because they were bullying me. We had this place where we would hang out that was part of an old movie theater where you could go have Cokes if you were a teenager. One evening we were thinking about whether any object could be an object of aesthetic appreciation or not. I took the latter position and made short work of the opposition. But from there, I started going off on a theory. It was the first time in my life I had ever done this, really thought for myself. Before I realized it, I had 15 people looking up at me sitting on a counter. There were my peers, the athletes, the good-looking people. And they were looking at me. I realized at that moment I was good at this teaching thing. So I knew one way or another I could do this. If I really went to town with an idea, people would listen.

I always knew I would learn, but I didn't know I would get an advanced degree. I was pretty active in the civil rights movement, so I thought I might take my talents into politics.

This was back in the 60s and a lot of things were going on. I was also active in the Peace and Freedom Party, seeking racial and social justice. I was involved in early feminism.

PSD: Who had the greatest influence on your formative years?

RB: I had a great English teacher who made Shakespeare come alive. His name was Fittipaldi and he had passion for the material. He embodied an emotional response to literature I had never seen before.

PSD: Though the 60s were a difficult time, it was also

a magical time of passion and involvement.

RB: It was a very exciting time compared to today.

PSD: There wasn't as much apathy back in those days.

RB: No, and there was a sense of purpose and potential for change. We really believed we were on the edge of a cultural revolution. We thought we were the generation that was going to bring about cataclysmic change. We were revolting not just about policies, but a way of life — a way of life in which some oppressed others. We could see it, but just seeing it somehow wasn't enough.

PSD: What do you think happened to that dream?

RB: I think it got co-opted by the engines of capitalism. I think it was cooking along pretty well but the promise of easy money was very seductive. It wasn't some sort of conspiracy or anything. I think the way in which that disillusionment occurred has been kind of a 'divide and conquer' thing. Interests got divided. We got fragmented. I think in some sense there might have been a loss of collective vision.

PSD: You work on campus. Do you see anything remotely like it used to be in terms of involvement, passion, and commitment?

RB: No, nothing like that—not since the 60s. The willingness on university campuses to shut the administration down, not only the belief, but the will to bring it off — there isn't anything like that.

PSD: Why do you think you approach teaching with such a passion?

RB: Because I see the classroom as an environment of mutual inquiry more than an environment for the transmission of inherited wisdom. I don't see the classroom as a vessel for the wisdom of the ancients. So I'm not as concerned with whether I have succeeded or failed in communicating these eternal truths to the students. I see the classroom as an opportunity where the student can also educate the teacher.

PSD: So the process is Socratic in nature?

RB: Well, I do conduct my classes in a very Socratic style. We try to put our heads in a certain place and inquire as to the nature of this thing together. I can learn from you because any set of joint inquirers can learn from each other.

PSD: Is it hard for you to use a grading system with students?

RB: One of the things I try to come to is that grades are not everything, but it is the process. The whole relationship with the instructor is based on trust and I hope to use the fruits of my experience and personal inquiry in a responsible way — to help other people to improve and to mature their own abilities and skills. So the grading process allows me in a very formal way to interact with you as a student, so that you may benefit from my experience. Grading can really be helpful in this context.

PSD: What qualities do you try to develop in your students?

RB: Intellectual health, in a very broad way. I'm using that notion, which is ancient and goes back to Plato's dialogues, that analogy between physical and intellectual health. This reminds us that health is not something you achieve once and then put in a drawer. It is an activity which has to be constantly maintained.

Why use a model like that? So often in modern education we tend to think of the course work that you do as having a beginning, a middle, and an end. You put it in a box and file it in the cerebral cortex, almost like the standards of currency exchange. It's something you possess, but not something you actually use anymore.

PSD: Like a degree?

RB: Like a degree. But health is not like that, health is not something you possess. It's something you practice. Health is something you have to live every day, which means you have to live a certain way. You have to have a certain sense of attitudes or habits you want to cultivate. As a teacher, I'm much more interested in helping people cultivate good habits that will be effective for them, rather than saying these are the truths or the facts that you should know.

PSD: Shouldn't one question everything to see if it has inner resonance?

RB: Oh yes, of course. Of course. You may know all the classical disciplines and what Plato said. But it doesn't mean you'll be able to think your way out of a paper bag.

Part of the role of an instructor is to give students basic knowledge, but you also have to train them to acquire skills so that they will be healthy. That something we all have—the thinking life—can be healthy or unhealthy. Just like your body.

PSD: Metaphorically, you are supplying software tools.

RB: Yes. What are your needs and what are your projects? Well, then, you will need tools that are appropriate to those projects. So you need to be tolerant and open minded, not just of beliefs, but of techniques. Techniques for thinking are not all the same.

PSD: Then there are experiences of instant awakening and spiritual enlightenment, satori!

RB: And those are amazingly more common as one gets older. It's an interesting sort of thing I've been thinking about. How many of these things were understandings of the world that I knew by phrases? They were there to be had, but now they are living things for me. I'm beginning to understand why the earlier thinkers, at least in the western tradition, made such a distinction between knowledge and wisdom. They insisted that it was experiential.

PSD: What advice would you offer someone with less experience than yourself?

RB: The old Socratic notion that you must learn to think for yourself. No one else can do your thinking for you. You must have your own reflective life if you want to capitalize on this sense of a difference between being knowledgeable and being wise. Being wise is something you can only have as an experience, you can't write it down. And don't stop when the phase makes sense. Maintain curiosity and a sense of tolerance of other views. Maintain a willingness to change your mind. Sometimes you will have insights that are worth keeping.

PSD: What about for a senior in high school or maybe a college student?

RB: I would guess at that age you already have a very healthy distrust of your elders and the best thing you can do is enrich it, maintain it, and feed it as best you can. Question authority, even the authority that tells you to question authority. This is a very special gift that human beings have. To be able to look at the inherited wisdom of the race and to question it. To suspect that it isn't any good unless it's my experience. To be able to do that means that we are more than instinctual beings. We don't have to behave like those who came before us. We can change the future of our culture, but we can't do that if we can't question.

There's a big difference between inherited knowledge and real experience. I think Thoreau said, "You cannot learn what you believe you already know." So a healthy disposition to have is a sense of your own ignorance. I find that the older I get, the less I know, although I am wiser. I am amazed at how much I do not know. You realize that wisdom is a way you live, not the things you say.

PSD: How would you define success?

RB: Continuing the experiment. Life is a grand experiment and to be successful is to continue it. Of course that means to continue to have an experimental spirit. To have lost that spirit would have been to be a failure. When you see life as a thought and as experimental, you are free to just keep trying different things. You are always learning. I engage in projects because I have questions.

PSD: For you it seems that the process is everything, that there is no big payday.

RB: That's what is meant by 'virtue is its own reward.' It's the activity that matters.

PSD: Are you a spiritual man?

RB: That's a pretty big question. Sometimes I'm so intoxicated by the beauty of music made by a composer like Bach, that it would be very difficult for me to say that I was not having a religious experience. That you became rapturous over something that was beyond you, something that is much, much bigger. If you are willing to extend the language of religiosity and spirituality to those sorts of experiences where the hair on the back of your neck stands up and you are in awe, intoxicated, rapturously infatuated with something incredibly beautiful and incredibly big. If that's what religious experience is, then certainly, I cultivate these regularly. They are some of the biggest kicks that I have. This is sort of non-standard talk.

PSD: Hopefully, this book will be full of non-standard talk.

RB: (Laughs) Also, I get really blissed out over mathematical ideas. I find them entrancing.

PSD: As I'm sure Stephen Hawking has on occasion.

RB: Yes. A kind of awe. Spirituality is passionate for me; it's not intellectual. It's not a matter of having true belief. For many people that's what spirituality is. It's involved in organizing, systematizing, and appreciating their beliefs. Whereas for me it's in the expression, the focusing, the concentration of passion. One can have a passion for ideas and have a spiritual kind of experience. I often think that many people are wrong in believing that they are spiritual when they are really looking through a window at spirituality wishing they were. But they don't know how to do it.

PSD: Was it not James Joyce who said, "Religion is a defense against having a religious experience?"

RB: Yes. You are imagining what it would be like to have the experience and mistaking imagination for actually having one. Religion is closer to what it is to be spiritual, and theology is closer to what it means to be knowledgeable. To be spiritual is to have a certain kind of experience. Those who have experienced the passion of ideas have a responsibility to their descendants to communicate that passion. Because if they fail to do so, it could come to an end and all it takes is one generation. It tells us how fragile culture is. Part of what we call spirituality is a recognition of the fragility.

PSD: You are a father. How about a personal definition of parental success?

RB: I think you know you're successful as a parent if you can still have deep, intimate, meaningful conversations with your children when they are 20. If you can still have a trusting, open, inquiring relationship of how you see the world, with the people whose diapers you changed. That is success.

PSD: What has worked for you in raising children?

RB: I think the most important thing as a parent is keeping a healthy attitude rather than making a new rule. "I need a new rule and then everything will be fine." This is a way that a lot of parents solve problems. This is pretty much the control model. My sense of having children is I invited them into the world. My wife and I took parts of each of us and invited this being into the world. This acknowledges the child as an autonomous being. Suppose you threw a party, invited people over, and started telling them how to live. You probably wouldn't have many friends.

PSD: Would you call that love?

RB: Sure, it's a kind of love. Love is a word in English which is about as vague as you can find. But it's interesting, given that vagueness is so attractive to philosophers, who love vague things. One needs to remember the games played with that word are very multifarious, and we need to be careful.

Carl Rowan
(New 20th Anniversary Content)

Backstory: The way this interview manifested is one of the most interesting stories that has occurred in my life. I'll try to be brief. Someone gave me the number to Carl's office, and I would call every couple of months to see if I could interview this iconic soul. His assistant Pam would graciously decline my requests and let me know that it wasn't me. Carl was just not doing interviews anymore. One afternoon in my music office I had this overwhelming feeling that I was supposed to call Mr. Rowan. I was reluctant to receive another 'no thanks,' but eventually opened my computer, looked at the number and dialed. To my shock Carl himself picked up. We chatted for a few minutes and he finally relented and agreed to meet. As we were about to hang up he asked, "By the way, how did you get my private home number?" I glanced at my screen and was utterly confused, since I only had access to his office. He then added, "Oh, never mind. I look forward to meeting you." We hung up and I felt like something magical and mysterious had unfolded. But I had to wonder, why? What happened at his home in Chevy Chase that day might offer some explanation.

PSD: What inspired you to go into writing?

CR: I had an English teacher in McMinnville named Mrs. Bessie, Mrs. Bessie Quinn, and she convinced me that I could write sonnets as good as Shakespeare. And I used to sit by a kerosene lamp in McMinnville writing ballads and sonnets up a storm. I remember I had a little crush on her daughter. And her husband, who was a truck driver or a grocer, said to me, "What do you hope to be?" I said, "Well, I write good poetry. I think I'll be a writer." He said, "Well, don't have any crush on my daughter, because my daughter's not marrying any damn boy."

PSD: He was smart.

CR: (Laughs) He was right, too.

PSD: At what point did you get interested in newspaper work?

CR: When I was in the Navy I became a Communications Officer. This is in World War II and of course, all the while I was reading all the newspapers I could get my hands on and especially the black newspapers which were the only ones carrying anything about the injustices of that period. And by the time I left the Navy I knew that I wanted to be a writer. So after going to Overland, where I paid close attention in my English class, I decided to go to a school of journalism to do post-graduate work. And I wound up at the University of Minnesota.

PSD: What you just said sounds almost easy. But when you did it, because of your color, it was not an automatic thing.

CR: You could count literally on the fingers of one hand the number of black Americans who had full-fledged jobs at a daily newspaper.

PSD: And also in the Navy, didn't you encounter some institutional resistance?

CR: Well, there had never been a Negro officer in the Navy ever in the country's history. And I became an officer and they said you couldn't serve on a ship and white officers would never let a black person in the ward room. But they were wrong. They said white sailors wouldn't take orders from a black guy. But I showed them they would.

PSD: You were one of the very first?

CR: I was one of the first 15.

PSD: What do you believe existed inside of you that created the strength to go and break all that new ground?

CR: Well, I haven't the faintest idea except that I

always had confidence in myself. And I guess that comes from being encouraged by my parents and by my grandmother and by teachers like Mrs. Quinn. When my mother said to me, "There can't be anybody in that room smarter than you are," I believed her, not knowing that mothers always feel this way about their children. But I believed it and then, of course, the way I grew up in McMinnville you had to be pretty tough. So whether it was playing first string end on the football team at 148 lbs. and having somebody say 'he's a tough little son-of-a-bitch,' or whether I was willing to fight some guy who insulted my sister. All of those things, I guess, create a spirit of toughness.

PSD: Yet you were able to stay tough but not become bitter.

CR: No, bitterness is a waste of time and brainpower. I learned long ago that if somebody hates you, if you reciprocate with hatred, you're destroying yourself more than they ever could.

PSD: When you got into journalism did you have it in your heart that you wanted to work on the civil rights issues and point out injustice?

CR: Well, I had made a vow when I left the Navy that I would do that. But I knew that wasn't all I wanted to do. I wanted to be a full-fledged journalist and write about everything. But I particularly wanted to say some things to the American people that I knew other journalists couldn't say because they hadn't had the experiences.

I left the Navy in '46 and this is when I made myself this pledge. I mean, I left the Navy as an 'officer and a gentleman,' as they say. So I get on this bus to go back to McMinnville and somebody wants me to sit in the back of the bus. Well, you know that's a lot of gall and crap. And I just felt that most Americans didn't understand the injustice and the horror of it all and particularly the lynching and the other deprivations of that era.

PSD: Do you think most prejudice comes from just simple ignorance and must be taught like it says in that old song from the show 'South Pacific,' you have to be taught to hate?

CR: Oh, that part of it is true and there are a lot of teachers out there, especially among politicians. I mean, that was a time where, if you were a southern politician, it was to your advantage to pit whites against blacks. And some still play the game.

PSD: The politics we see today is based on fear. People trying to manipulate people.

CR: Well, when people don't know each other, they tend to fear. I mean if you put a big fence up, a big wall up between you and me, I'm going to wonder what you're doing on the other side of the wall and how you're plotting against me to do what. That's what segregation did.

PSD: Did you have much experience with Martin Luther King personally?

CR: Oh yes.

PSD: What do you remember about him?

CR: I think, most of all, that he was brilliantly articulate in expressing the aspirations, not just of black people, but of the oppressed people everywhere and he got to the consciousness of America. I was in the meeting in Montgomery where the bus boycott was planned.

PSD: It has always amazed me that the catalyst for monumental change can come from just a simple action or event, like a woman on a bus, Miss Rosa Parks, deciding not to move her seat.

CR: Well, one person can move mountains. But don't forget also that, despite the force and all the publicity of that boycott, it didn't end until the U.S. Supreme Court ruled. So the rule of law was very important in bringing that to a conclusion when they outlawed segregation on the buses of Montgomery.

PSD: You remind me of another great American, Justice Thurgood Marshall, who was deeply involved in that ruling as well as others.

CR: Oh yes. Especially in that particular case. He was an amazing man and I wrote his biography.

PSD: You were at the central core of a group that created tremendous change in America.

CR: Well, in the role as just about the only black journalist they knew, I made quite a difference. No other journalist could have been admitted to the house where they were holding that meeting where they planned the boycott. I read an interesting article in one of the journal reviews recently, asking, "Was it proper for blacks to cover blacks?" I said, "What the hell is this? Whites have been covering whites from time eternal."

PSD: How do you feel about race relations in this moment?

CR: We still have some grievous problems. It's infinitely better than when I grew up in Tennessee, but there still are a myriad of injustices.

PSD: Do you think there will ever come a day, maybe

not in your life or even mine, where our skin pigmentation won't really matter?

CR: I don't think we'll ever see the day when race doesn't matter.

PSD: It's just an inherent human condition?

CR: I think so.

PSD: That's sad.

CR: Very sad. But all the evidence of human history supports it. And I'm not just talking about this country. We look at various kinds of conflict that have existed around the world for eons.

PSD: If not race, perhaps it would be religion.

CR: Oh yes, absolutely.

PSD: I know it's a big question, but what is it in the human nature that needs to say, "I'm better than you?"

CR: Well, I guess we all have one kind of insecurity or another to one degree or another. And there seems to be something in the genes that says to somebody to be suspicious of that person who looks different.

PSD: Or calls his God a different name.

CR: Or acts differently.

PSD: But yet you feel called, and in my own small way so do I, that even if it's hopeless, we must try to make a difference regardless of any chance for success.

CR: We've got to and it does make a huge difference. Otherwise we'll destroy each other. We have to follow that calling and be courageous. That's why we do what we do.

PSD: You've always had a place in your heart for the

underdog, at least in all the columns I've read.

CR: There are a lot of voiceless people without any clout in society. And the measure of justice in that society depends on how many people there are who are willing to take a stand for those underdogs.

PSD: Any thought on our political system and how it could be changed to better serve the masses rather than the privileged few?

CR: Campaign financing is the greatest scandal in America. Also, one of the worrisome things is this current trend of having people start up militias and all kinds of hate groups based on the assumption that the federal government is the enemy, or the federal government is the friend of the people I hate. That's what is so destructive about the revelations about the Branch Davidian Compound in Waco. When you get the federal government caught in a lie or holding back the truth or possible conspiracy, it feeds these arguments of the hate groups that they need all kinds of guns and bombs and so forth in their possession so they can protect the people from their government. So we're in a very, very tough situation these days.

PSD: What do you think of our country with all its amazing wealth and material prosperity and so many without healthcare and without even adequate nutrition?

CR: I think it's criminal. But it's a crime against humanity and we'll pay for it one way or the other. In fact, we do pay for it now. People rant and rave about street crime and births out of wedlock and the cost of poverty programs, etc. Well, those are the things that flow out of economic injustice and they militate against a society ever being as great as it could be.

PSD: What would you tell a young man or woman reading this who said, "I want to make a difference in this world"?

CR: First, I would tell them you've got to start out with knowledge. You've got to know what's going on. I say to youngsters you've got to read because if you don't read you can't write because you won't know anything to write. And if you can't write in this society and speak, you can't have much of an impact. I mean, that was one of the great things about Martin Luther King. He could speak and he could write.

Second, I put my mind to work and ask, "Does this make sense?" And if it makes sense, I let me heart follow. And I may ask for a little advice along the way.

PSD: So a strong foundation in education.

CR: Yes. And the ability to communicate and then you have to have guts. You may have to find a way so you aren't worried every day about where the next meal is coming from. That's why I've always had at least four jobs at one time, so no one son-of-a-bitch could threaten me.

I ran a scholarship program and I said to these youngsters, "If you look around at the people who have had a great impact on human endeavors, you will find that they all could communicate magnificently."

PSD: Talk about the scholarship programs you started.

CR: I picked up The Washington Post one day and saw that black students at McKinley High School here refused to stand when their names were called for the honor roll. They didn't want their peers to know they worked and studied hard enough to make the honor roll. This just dismayed me and I thought about it and I said, "There must be some kind of reward that would make these youngsters say to their peers, I don't care what you think of me, I want that reward." So I took $32,000 of my own money, and asked my friends to match it, so that I could give out some scholarships. I got 16 and I asked them to put up 16. Well, actually they responded so that the first year I had $280,000 for scholarships. We started this program, Project Excellence, in which the kids write an essay. First they have to be nominated by their high school and write an essay. And then they come into orals before 10 judges and we reward the ones who show excellence and the greatest disdain for their know-nothing peers. And since then, the program has grown. In the last few years we've given away between $3 and $4 million each year. Since 1987, we've give over 3,000 youngsters more than $57 million.

PSD: How does it make you feel when you see someone who has come through that program?

CR: Oh man, at the dinner—not just me—but at these dinners, at some point there's not a dry eye in the house. I look out and people are balling. Tears are running down my face and it's just absolutely moving. And the thing is, I can't count over two youngsters that somebody might say is not a success.

PSD: You wife just came by and said hello. How long have you been married?

CR: 49 years.

PSD: Now that's a different form of success.

CR: Oh yes.

PSD: What makes a successful marriage and how do you create one that will last?

CR: I don't know. It may be a form of bigotry, but I still think of divorce as failure and I think it takes a lot of patience. When I hear somebody say, my wife and I have never had an argument, I know that's the biggest lie I've ever heard. Because my wife and I may have had one or two or three every day for 49 years. (Laughs)

But it also goes back to the business of respecting other people. And no matter how many columns I write in which I speak with a certainly as to my wisdom, I know that I had to respect somebody who can put up with me for 49 years. So that's the first formula. Find somebody whose opinions you can respect and whose behavior you can respect. And then be patient. (Laughs)

PSD: How do you personally define success?

CR: I would say that success is when achievements reasonably approximate dreams. It doesn't matter how simple or grandiose those dreams may be, but your mind and your heart set the benchmarks and if you come close to those, you have achieved success no matter what anybody else thinks.

PSD: What are some of the qualities that a human being should try to develop and embody to have a better chance at that sort of success?

CR: Well, I think around the top of my list is a feeling that in some way you're showing personal courage. If you can say, in the whole context of civil rights for example, I want on my tombstone these words, "He never sold out." That is a great beginning.

PSD: Does it take a lot of courage to not sell out?

CR: Absolutely. I remember when I was in the state

department, working like hell to change things, one of my great allies was Ed Merle and I got offered a really good job. Money I thought I couldn't turn down. And I said to Ed Merle, "I'm going to be leaving." He said, "You can't go." I said, "Why not?" He said, "Because there won't be a dry eye in the state department."

PSD: You're a huge advocate of gun control?

CR: Yes. Well, I tell you, the violence around schools is simply a reflection of a very violent society. You know, this is a violent society and it always has been. It was born in violence, sustained in violence, and there is no way in the world you're going to preach Hollywood out of making movies full of violence and gratuitous violence at that. The attitude of so many people is that, if you're in a dispute, people tend to settle it with violence. The kids pick that up and I just frankly don't know how you turn that around.

PSD: What was your biggest break?

CR: My biggest break was finding a $20 bill on the day I was dropping out of Tennessee State and having the Navy decide a few days later that it would allow Negroes to take the national exam for officer's training, and a professor, Merle Epps at Tennessee State, dragooning me into taking the exam. And I passed and got the commission into the Navy.

PSD: So you were going to drop out?

CR: I had no choice.

PSD: Why you were out of money?

CR: I didn't have the $20 to pay the next quarter's tuition.

PSD: You found $20?

CR: I went down to the Greasy Spoon with my buddy Joe Bates. And as we walked back, something said that one of those green wads, you see they threw away their green transfers when they got off the dinky bus, and something said one of those green wads you just passed was not a bus transfer. I picked it up and it was a $20 bill. I went right up and paid my tuition.

PSD: What do you think that something was that said that?

CR: I wouldn't even speculate. There are people who want me to say it was God.

PSD: You have to have some feeling?

CR: All I am sure of is that some student on his or her way to pay tuition had lost it.

PSD: But something told you to look and that's something that if we sit down with normal physics we wouldn't be able to really explain.

CR: That's right. Well, there are a lot of things you can't explain.

PSD: Do you have a spiritual faith?

CR: Oh yes. I wouldn't have a scholarship program if I didn't. But I regard religion as something quite different from the structured stuff that most people talk about.

PSD: I would be more curious about it in a spiritual sense rather than a dogmatic sense. More mystical in nature, it is beyond the mind.

CR: That's the kind of religion I'm involved in. Yes, and something told me to go back and look in the weeds. There are a lot of forces at work that we don't understand and probably never will. (Pauses and starts to cry)

PSD: Maybe, by the same mysterious element some people refer to as God, that said turn around and look for the $20, has also guided you in your work at times.

CR: I can't say that. Or maybe I have been guided and have not been aware of it at that particular time. But I can tell you that there is something to sitting. You know, there are days when it's harder than others to decide on a topic for a column and there are days when suddenly a light will go on and I'll know that there's something that I've just got to talk about, and it seems as though I'm spiritually guided to that subject.

Well, you know, it wasn't just finding a $20 bill. It was also being in Merle Epps's history class, and he had a reputation for being a real mean son-of-a-bitch. And two days after I paid my tuition, I'm sitting there and he's unexplainably late. And he walked into the room and he said, "Carl Rowan, come with me to the Dean's office."

PSD: Why do you think we're here? Have you ever thought about that in, what, 74 years?

CR: I think we're here to do more than eat and drink and procreate, to do more than survive. I mean every time I see something like this hurricane coming, I visualize myself out in space and you look at this here globe and you get a whole different concept than just sitting here. And you look, and there's this little, tiny, fragile planet. And Christ, it looks like it's boiling up from the inside. And you get the earthquake in Turkey, and water is boiling over and you get this thing coming out of the oceans, you get floods and you say, boy, we've got a lot of work to do to save this planet and to save each other and that we're charged with doing more than simply existing for three score and ten.

PSD: What role does love play in all of this?

CR: Oh, love is the beginning and the end of it all. If you can't love anybody, you can't really function. You can't have a decent life.

PSD: How would you like to be remembered? Do you ever think about that sort of thing?

CR: "He never sold out."

Shankaracharya Swami

"If one has peace, if one has love, if one can live in dignity, if one can accept what life presents and bring awareness and love into every situation — then I would say that they were successful."

Preceptor, Sadhana Ashram

Backstory: I heard from a friend that someone had created a small ashram on the outskirts of Nashville a few miles from my own home. I went by and immediately felt a connection to the Swami, a man from the west who had found enlightenment in the east. Shank, as we affectionately called him had a wicked sense of humor and a keen eye for insights. I spent hours with him conversing, meditating, and sharing meals. He was always very generous with me and anyone who came his way in search of answers. Shank also loved my dog, constantly pointing out that he was a true Master because he was always 100% present in the moment. The ashram never caught on there in the Bible Belt, so the group migrated west to California.

PSD: How did you come to adopt an eastern way of life?

SS: When I was younger, I was on a quest for greater knowledge. I worked in aerospace engineering and design at the time. I actually worked on a system for the Apollo moon flight and helped design it. Even though I was discovering more and more about mechanical things, I still felt somewhat dry in my own experience of life, of touching something that would really give me fulfillment. I wanted to know why people did things, what their motivations were, and to get more into the human heart — to understand at a deeper level.

PSD: Was this during the 1960s?

SS: This was a time in the mid-'60s when the psychedelic movement was flourishing. People were looking for answers, for something more. The next logical step was to look for masters, or people that had found a way to be able to stay in steady states of awareness. Through their spiritual practices, they were able to attain something deeper within themselves. The psychedelic period showed other possibilities in consciousness, but it was difficult to find anyone who was really able to have a positive transformation through the experience. I was looking for people whose lives reflected a deep state of spiritual experience, regardless of their religious context or spiritual approach.

PSD: Did you undertake a spiritual quest?

SS: I started wandering the world looking for people that had found some kind of spiritual fulfillment. Generally, I was looking for saints in different traditions and different places. I just wanted to spend time with them and see what kind of effect it would have on me, hoping that it would counter the dryness I felt inside.

PSD: You went from an external model of fulfillment to an internal model.

SS: Originally, I was looking for fulfillment through my career or trying to climb the ladder into a good position. But the ideas of 'Who am I?', of divine love, or of feeling a oneness with everyone else were still within me. I wasn't able to attain those things through my career. I wandered through Africa, Europe, and the Middle East. Eventually, I wound up in India.

In India, the basic context is that divinity dwells within all beings. The culture is based on the belief of honoring the God within you and the other. The idea of the spiritual path is to remove whatever it is within you that obscures that divinity within, so that you can realize it or become one with it. It's just like where the Bible says, "The kingdom of heaven dwells within."

PSD: Did you find common traits among the varied traditions?

SS: Even though I spent time with a number of saints from a number of traditions, I started to notice that they all possessed the same characteristics. Even though they had different approaches, there still was a spiritual energy that could be felt there. There was still love and compassion, and they had come into some experience of love. This was a love that embraced the whole world and all situations. So by spending time with these saints and patterning after them, I was able to tap into things that I wasn't able to tap into merely by reading books. They all taught universal principles, even if they did so within different frameworks.

PSD: What are these universal principles?

SS: The first principle is that love is inherent within all beings. People are always looking outside of themselves to find love. They may find it for awhile, but the situation may change and then there is sorrow. Actually, the situation outside is only an occasion for love to flash forward from within a person. Most people don't realize that love is their own inner treasure. If they can find it within themselves, then love can radiate outward into everything they do, and isn't dependent on the external situation or a relationship.

The other principle is unity. We are not really separate. Eastern belief is that the supreme consciousness manifests in different guises. In some it is more revealed, and in others, more concealed.

Everything in the universe is connected. If we find love in our selves and also realize that this is one sea of consciousness with different individual manifestations in it, we can create a whole different way in which we look at the world and other people.

Actually, the great saints and masters like Jesus or Buddha are people who realized divine love and experienced it within themselves, thus manifesting it in the world. They became examples for others to pattern on to come into that same experience.

PSD: These great beings were completely self-actualized.

SS: Jesus was someone who experienced that divinity within and manifested it forth into the world. But it doesn't mean that a Muslim or a Jew doesn't have divinity or awareness within him. A Christian can pattern on Jesus, and because of his state of being, can hopefully bring forth the same qualities. These great beings and religions are not here to divide people. If you start out with the idea that divinity dwells within all people and can be honored, then the potential for self-actualization is there for all people regardless of their religious belief.

PSD: The key is to believe you are not separate from the Divine?

SS: Instead of thinking divinity is out there somewhere in God or a God-like being, bring it to where it is part of one's own self. If we could do this, it would break down the friction between a lot of people. Even if we did not agree with the way they were trying to manifest divinity, we could still honor it.

PSD: Isn't one's ultimate experience with the Divine

unique, and also especially difficult to communicate?

SS: The experience of Divine love and unity manifests through one's own field of karma or one's nature in its own unique way. But it is the same love and the same inner self. If light passes through different glasses it has different colors, but is still the same light. The universal love and principles that we come into communion will express themselves through our nature in a way that appears to be unique because of the display. But the love is still the same.

PSD: In its infinite manifestations, it's still the same light?

SS: That's right. In certain ways, you have to look at life as a school that we're all looking to learn something from. We're looking for peace, happiness, and understanding, and going to a great school. There are a lot of experiences that can be difficult, like suffering and pain, but they can be vehicles for one to learn greater tolerance and compassion. It's not the situation, but how one looks at the situation, and how one deals with and is affected by the situation.

PSD: It's a matter of what we choose to embrace.

SS: There can be certain thoughts that enter the mind. The thoughts themselves can't really do anything to the person. It's how one looks at the thoughts, and how one judges the thoughts. Which thoughts does one choose to empower? What we are doing here is trying to help one use life situations to help bring spiritual transformation and growth. We also try to help one make friends with the mind and not to have identifications that would detract from their own innate radiance that dwells within them, which is joy and bliss.

PSD: Are joy and bliss our natural state?

SS: The source of all things is within your own being. If one can contact that loving place within themselves, it will radiate into all their situations. If they have love within themselves, they can see love in others. So one good way to help the world is to find joy and love within oneself and bring that into the world.

PSD: The influence of one vital person can be tremendous.

SS: That's right. The sense is of awe and wonder, not one of power.

PSD: So it's not an ego-oriented experience?

SS: No. We are all manifestations of the One, if we realize that the ego has a different connotation. Because everywhere we look is a display of the One. So we don't have the sense of individual separateness that divides us and puts us in competition with other people. Or even seeing other people as 'other'. That's different from the ego that sees itself as separate. How will you treat someone you see as part of your own divinity? It's a whole different consciousness. The way to bring about harmony and peace in the world is for the divinity to be revealed rather than concealed. God dwells in all beings.

PSD: How do we find inner divinity while we are in this human form?

SS: The way to find it does not come from a set of rules or a set of techniques. The first thing to recognize is simply that it's there, that the love dwells within.

PSD: What if I'm skeptical, but searching anyway?

SS: Use the rational mind. For example, say you love

your girlfriend. Five minutes later, you find out she slept with your friend. All of a sudden, you don't feel the same love. But your girlfriend is exactly the same as five minutes ago. Only the way you looked at her has changed. So the love didn't come from the girlfriend. She was an occasion where love flashed forward from within yourself. It's logical. Love dwells within and everyone has had experiences of that love. What the mystic is trying to do is tap the love within and radiate that into all experience.

There are many religions, spiritual techniques, paths, and approaches to doing this. However, the fundamental task is to first recognize that 'It' is indeed there. The second is to want to come into the experience of it. Because if there is a want and there is a will, then there is a way. If the intent is there, and the recognition is there, then the way opens for that to happen.

PSD: Will consciousness find us if we seek it?

SS: Yes, because it is the One who appears as the yearning and the One who fulfills the yearning.

PSD: In the end, is it all just consciousness at play?

SS: Yes. That's the whole deal. Have an honest yearning and the recognition that love dwells within you. Be aware of the air that literally connects you to another. One has to court unity and court love.

PSD: God is a mask or metaphor for the Oneness of all creation?

SS: It could be looked at that way. You can embrace the world, but you have to be careful not to lose your connection to divinity. To embrace means that you are not detached from the world around you. The key is to practice both detachment and embracing simultaneously.

PSD: What inspired you to create an ashram?

SS: We are basically looking to present an environment that people will come into, that will help things to come forth from within oneself. I'm not necessarily telling anyone how it all is. I don't even pretend to know how it all is. To consider some of these possibilities opens a person to more flexibility and tolerance.

PSD: How would you define success?

SS: Real success has to do with divine love and unity, with finding something within yourself to bring into your life that helps make the world a better place. To help bring about a feeling of love, compassion, and deeper understanding. One could be a successful carry-out boy at Kroger. People could have their groceries carried out and by just coming into contact with this boy, there could be some light brought into their lives because of his attitude. They might say, "Look at that guy carrying the groceries. He seems to be more happy and have more joy than I do, and I am a millionaire."

PSD: Yet I don't see you diminishing achievement.

SS: There is something great about reaching a lofty position or going to the top in one's chosen endeavor that is not to be diminished. It's an accomplishment. At the same time, it's really important that one does not sacrifice the roots of one's being.

If deeper understanding and compassion can come forth in one's life, then I would think that to be a great success, regardless of the person's status — whether they have cancer or AIDS, work as a carry-out man, or they are the President. If one has peace, if one has love, if one can live in dignity, if one can accept what life presents and bring awareness and love into every situation — then I would say that they were successful.

PSD: In our culture, we have achieved a great deal on the material plane.

SS: It's a double-edged sword. Material wealth and all that goes with it has its beauty. At the same time, there are all kinds of problems and sufferings. I see that everywhere and in the people who come here every day. The material things are nice, but you have to find the thread within yourself to give your life resonance. You can get so caught up in the rat race, you fail to see all the beauty around you.

PSD: I know you don't identify with your form, but how would you like people to remember the experience of your physical manifestation?

SS: I'm just part of a process. Being a spiritual teacher, what I teach is that the spiritual teacher dwells within all people as their higher intuition. I'm here to help turn people inward so they can realize that within themselves.

PSD: You are a spiritual facilitator?

SS: For me, it's just being part of a process to help someone discover more of what is within themselves. If I can help with that, if that's what is happening, it's a great thing. I don't take any credit for it. It's just happening.

PSD: Yet it's nice to be part of it.

SS: It's nice to add my life to the current of unity and love. Life is a beautiful thing. There is a lot of suffering, but within this dance there is a divinity. To be able to dance in a beautiful way through whatever situations might occur, and bring awareness into them, with poise, is a great thing. Hopefully, that's what is happening here.

Governor Don Sundquist
(New 20th Anniversary Content)

Don Sundquist served as the 47th Governor of Tennessee from 1995 to 2003. Prior to that, he represented Tennessee's 7th congressional district in the United States House of Representatives from 1983 to 1995.

Backstory: I had the good fortune of meeting the Governor when I was booked to play the piano at his official Christmas party out at the Governor's mansion. He and his wife Martha could not have been nicer. Later, I was invited back a few times to visit. Don was a down-to-earth guy and easy to talk to. He didn't strike me as political type at all. We had lunch several times and became casual friends. He agreed to be in the book immediately, but his staff couldn't seem to nail down a date for me to see him. Then one night I ran into him and Martha at the movies with him asking, "What happened to that interview we were supposed to do?" When I told him he took out a small pocket journal and made note. The next morning I got a call from his staff asking me if I could come in on Monday and see the Governor. Sometimes you need a little luck to make things happen.

PSD: Talk about your life and growing up.

GS: My parents were wonderful. I'm the first in my family to graduate high school or college. My father had to quit school during the depression and get a job. My mother lived out in the country, and at the end of the 8th grade they felt she was too sickly to walk into town and go to school. Yet she ran businesses. She can add a column of figures faster than you can on a handheld computer. I had a grandmother who was just tenacious and insisted that I was going to do something in life and that I go to college. She would 'throw a fit' if I didn't do what she told me to do. So once I got started in college I liked it and found out I could do well.

PSD: What drew you into the public service sector?

GS: I've always liked history and civics. I grew up in Illinois and it was kind of ironic. We had a mock election in college in 1956 and I was a Tennessee delegate. I've never talked about this before today I don't think. And it was a democratic convention! I was a conformer delegate. I look back on that and it's fortuitous. Here I end up Tennessee!

I believe that we have a system in America that is the best in the world. Anybody can be anything they want to be if they're willing to pay the price. And if you succeed, you have an obligation to put something back in the system. So I got involved in politics because I felt it was important to have a comparative two-party system in this state. Howard Baker has been my mentor. I helped Howard in the '64 campaign in Shelbyville at winning there, and again in '66. I was also his youth chairman in '72, if you would believe it. I believe in public service. It's important to put something back in the system that has allowed me to prosper.

PSD: So service is important to you?

I think public service is important. What's critical for the continued success of our system is to have people from all walks of life get involved in making a contribution in the community. Now it can take many forms. It can be in civic affairs, it can be in politics, or just improving the system. So I ran for Congress. Nobody gave us a chance and we won. I ran for Governor and won that. So it's been a real privilege for me to be in public service and public life, and I've loved every minute of it.

PSD: You obviously believe the individual can make a difference. Because I think running for office is saying,

'I think I can have an impact.'

GS: Yes. That's what separates this country from other countries. One person can make a big difference. Like the man, when his son Adam was kidnapped and killed, who started "America's Most Wanted."

PSD: John Walsh.

GS: Yes, John Walsh. His son was Adam. You can just look everywhere. People from all walks of life make a difference. And one of the things I worry about in politics is that the system is increasingly moving toward the model that only people of wealth are running for office. That shouldn't be the way it is. We need people in office who represent all walks of life. We have to be careful within our system that we make it possible for anybody to run. I mean, you look back to the Continental Congress and people from all walks of life were involved. They don't ask you what color you are or what your background is or what you do for a living when it comes time to defend your country. We are unique and we have something very special. And if we don't embellish it, protect it, and enhance it, it can slip away from us.

PSD: With all the money pouring into and through the system, how do we protect the less fortunate who don't have the money or influence of the special interest groups?

GS: I think you have to do it through a strong two-party system. The party can be the vehicle for anybody to run. If only millionaires can fund their campaigns then we're in real trouble. That's not the way the system is supposed to work. That also means we've got to have people participating in city councils, road commissioners, county executives, general assemblies, you know, every step along the way. We have to have participation in the process from all kinds of people, because the diversity of elected officials ought to be there and it ought to be reflective of the country.

PSD: In your latest tax proposal you will try to shift some of the strain off of the lower income families towards those that have a lot more material wealth.

GS: It's going to be tough, too.

PSD: They're already lining up against you as we speak.

GS: Yes, the vested interests. There's nothing wrong with vested interests and there's nothing wrong with lobbying as long as everybody can speak up. In Tennessee we have developed a tax system where certain professions and certain groups of people are paying virtually no taxes. There's something wrong when you have a group of professionals, and I'm not picking on one, paying virtually no taxes.

PSD: Give me some examples.

GS: Professionals who don't charge. There's no sales tax on their services whether it's an accountant or a doctor or a lawyer or a dentist or an advertising agency. There's no sales tax on their services and, for the most part, the tax system that we had is based on profit or major investment in equipment.

PSD: Then you have a segment of the population with very limited resources paying hundreds of dollars a year in sales tax on groceries alone.

Exactly. You have many people who are on fixed incomes working, or elderly on fixed income that have to make a choice between food and medicine. So you have a government that has to provide certain services and functions to businesses and people of the state. When you have certain business people who are paying no taxes, while you have every family paying taxes on groceries, that's not fair.

Now you have a whole segment of businesses, service industry kind of people, that are trying to be convinced to pay their share and, at the same time, relieve the pressure on people who pay a little bit of taxes. But it's a lot to them in terms of survival as a family. So a lot of people say, "Well, you're not acting like a Republican."

PSD: By championing the interests of the less fortunate?

GS: Well, I'm acting like my kind of Republican. I think Republicans have a reputation for being uncaring.

PSD: Usually being a Republican is stereotypically associated with being for big business and against things like the working poor or the environment.

GS: Yet Teddy Roosevelt was an environmentalist. Why would we concede this as a party? Of the environment to the other party? And by the way, we shouldn't. I'm an environmentalist and the air and the water in Tennessee are the cleanest they have been in 25 years.

PSD: Hopefully one's moral compass would take precedence over an abstract political label.

GS: Yes. I said in my last campaign that I'm going to do what's right. I'm going to do what's fair and I'm never going to run for office again. So I have an opportunity to do some things that need to be done, and some people are going to think it's going to hurt the Republican party short-term. Long-term I think it's going to show people that we are a party of compassion, that we believe every citizen 'has a right and opportunity to be anything they want to be or do anything they want to do,' and we can do so with compassion. We're not the party of big business, if you look at individuals...

PSD: You don't have a boss.

GS: The party is like my boss.

PSD: But it can't tell you what to do.

GS: No, it can't. But I think our party has had an unjust reputation, an unfair reputation for not caring, and I think people will look upon our party in the future for what we are.

PSD: People caring and compassion are nice words to hear on any level, especially politically. As the head of the 'state ship,' you must be concerned about the ones left behind.

GS: The next task is to find those who are the toughest to educate, the toughest to employ and the toughest to train. That's going to take special attention. We're going to have to work on learning disabilities. It's going to be a slow but achievable goal. Education is where it's really at and so what we're spending a lot of money on in Tennessee. Governor McWhortor spent a lot of time and committed a lot of money there and we're doing the same thing K-12.

PSD: What advice would you give a young student to succeed in school?

GS: I would say, study hard, read a lot, learn to read and put something back in the system that helps your community and know that you can be anything you want to be. I just saw a wonderful movie the night before, "October Sky." Have you seen the movie?

PSD: Yes, I loved it.

GS: It's about the book called, "Rocket Ball." I went out and bought the book. It was filmed in Tennessee; filmed in Oliver Springs and Knoxville. I think it exemplifies what our children in this state ought to see. They ought to see that movie and know it doesn't matter who or what you are. If you have some goals that you've set, you can do it. I mean, it's getting easier now because we have a better educational system. But you have to do things that take some discipline.

PSD: Like you said earlier, "Be willing to pay the price."

GS: You've got to pay the price and it takes some discipline. I mean, I have worked since I was about 12 or 13 years old. I had a paper route and sold soft drink bottles at grocery stores. I also sold Christmas trees or whatever and my grandmother taught me to save. You make a dime, you save a penny. So you have to save. You have to know when to invest money, and it may be an investment in education or it may be an investment in a computer. What I tell children is to study hard and set some goals. Lamar Alexander said, "Aim for the top. It's much brighter there." There's a lot of truth in that.

PSD: On a personal level, how would you define success?

GS: Success is internal. You define what you would like to do and be in life. And for some it may be a family and a good living or even a hobby. For others, maybe they want to be President of the United States. You can be successful by doing anything if that's what you aspire to do and be. People are not a failure just because they're not in the public eye or they're not President of the United States.

PSD: Or if they don't make a lot of money.

GS: Or if they don't make a lot of money. The most important thing is your health. If you have your health, you have everything. If you don't have your health, you don't have anything. My father-in-law pointed that out to me early on. But set some goals for yourself and strive to make those goals. For some families it's making sure their children get a good education and get a good start in life. That's their goal and that's fine. For others it may be climbing Mt. Everest. That's a goal and everything they do is aimed toward that. For another person it may be forming a Trail Club and cleaning up the trails in the Smokies, and they spend all their time and energy doing that. So success is how you define it within yourself.

PSD: Or being elected Governor?

GS: Well, I never thought I would be Governor of the state of Tennessee. When I was young, that's not what…I didn't know what I wanted to do. But I wanted to do something well.

PSD: What do you do to stay grounded?

GS: I hope I haven't changed. I have friends. It's having people who will say the truth and saying, hey, you're off base. We sit around this room most mornings for an hour or two and I have a great staff and anybody can speak up and say, hey, that's crazy. You have to depend on people. You have to trust people. You have to have friends. Most of my friends were my friends before I started in politics and after I was elected. They will still be my friends when I leave office and go back wherever we're going to live.

PSD: You're talking about people who care about you and not your position in life.

GS: That's it. The people who are making you feel

important now, most of them when you're gone from office, they're not going to be your friends. It's the people who were your friends before who are going to be your friends after. So you have to understand that and I think that's why a lot of people miss being in public office. Because they're so devastated when they leave that they don't understand.

PSD: That a lot of the attention and praise they received while in office was false?

GS: It's false attention. So I think it's a perspective. It's having friends and understanding the real values in life.

PSD: What brings you the most joy in your life?

GS: Making a difference. Changing things for the future in Tennessee. That brings me a lot of joy. Also, being with my granddaughter gives me a lot of joy. So it's not just public. Some of these things can be private in the satisfaction in your family. We're a close family and we vacation together and we call each other everyday or so. So there's not one thing that makes me happy in life. There's a whole series of things. I do hurt for people when they have problems. I feel bad for them when they lose a family member. I don't understand meanness. How anybody can be mean to a child. Like, how can somebody hook someone up and pull him or her along the road behind a car? I don't understand that. I think we, as Americans, have to speak up and say that's not acceptable behavior in this country.

What we can do for children, the least of us, is important. Somebody told me a long time ago, and I'll tell you who it was, he played the violin in Israel.

PSD: Isaac Stern?

GS: Yes, Isaac Stern. He went to Carnegie Hall when I was in Congress. He said, "You know, we bring children into the world and you see them and you hold them and they have love. They don't have hate. They're not mad at anybody. They're not angry with anybody. But we inflict upon them diseases, we inflict upon them behavioral problems, we teach them to hate. These children are born into life loving."

He's right. So what can we do to help people continue to love each other and not hate? What can we do to create an opportunity for them in their lives that will be greater than the opportunities we've had? I think that's the ticket we have to buy for our own life. We have to invest something to make life better for others.

PSD: That's a very beautiful and humanistic view, Don. How do we build that bridge?

GS: I think by example.

PSD: You've got to live it.

GS: You've just got to live it. What made Mother Teresa successful? One of the things I've noticed in America is we don't have heroes like we used to. You know, Hank Aaron may be a great guy, but I never will forgive him for not signing autographs for some kids, including my son one time. We're paying these people an inordinate amount of money for their athletic skills. They owe something to the system, to the children. So as Governor I try to never walk by a group of kids without talking to them or signing something for them.

PSD: When we go the extra mile for someone, it makes such a difference.

GS: I think we all have to do this. We need to create

heroes. We need to spend the time and heroes can be anyone. Anyone can be Mother Teresa. That's what matters most. I'm an optimist and I believe things will continue to get better. Maybe that's the wrong attitude, but I think things are going to get better. It's not about equipment or machinery. In the end, it's all about people.

PSD: When it's all said and done and you leave the earth, how would you like to be remembered?

GS: Well, we will all be off the earth.

PSD: Yes, in fifty years or so. It's a short life.

GS: Yes. People are going to say, "Who?" (Laughs)

PSD: Yes, but if someone could recall you.

GS: I guess I would like to be remembered like Austin Peay. Like Austin Peay, he made a change in the state of Tennessee for the good.

PSD: Maybe as a parent too and a good grandfather too?

GS: Oh yes, all of that. But most of all, a good family person. I was raised that way.

PSD: Family is real important to you?

GS: It is.

John Seigenthaler

"I would like to be known as a journalist who made a difference, but also as a father who made a difference. I would also like to be remembered as someone who made a small difference in the field of civil rights and worked in other ways to right civil wrongs."

President, First Amendment Center and Chairman

Emeritus, The Tennessean

Backstory: During my interview with John he kept stonewalling me on his feelings and bombarding with anecdotes and old stories. After about 90 minutes of this I said I was going to start the tape over and we could try again. He exploded with laughter and then we dove deeper. When he talked about his brother, he got very emotional. After we were finished he invited me to lunch and a beautiful friendship began. When he invited Bill Moyers to town, I had the privilege of meeting Bill and he even interviewed for my book. Later, John invited me on his fabulous show, 'A Word on Words,' to help promote the book. We stayed in touch, we had lunch, I would drop by his office and we would discuss the world. He was just a wonderful, generous guy. When I gave him a copy of my book, 'Hitchhiking With Larry David,' he read it in one night. He called me the next day with praise, encouragement and affirmation. A little while later I was back on his show for what was easily my all-time favorite interview appearance. Like many, I loved and admired John and his passing was a huge loss.

PSD: When did you first fall in love with words?

JS: Pretty early on, in the sixth, seventh, and eighth grades. I had the same wonderful teacher all three years, a nun, who told me I could write poetry, essays, and short stories. I loved words and continued to through high school. My mother and father both read to me from the first days that I can remember. I remember getting a record of Sir Lawrence Olivier doing Hamlet and Henry V, and I memorized every word. I could probably still recite a soliloquy or two.

PSD: What drew you into the newspaper business?

JS: I really wanted to be a teacher, thinking I would have been good at it. But my uncle got me a job at The Tennessean, and I got hooked as a reporter. It was clearly the right thing for me. I never thought about doing anything else after I had been there a short time. Ironically, the first lead paragraph I ever wrote didn't even have a verb in it. (He laughs.)

PSD: Can you tell me a little about the First Amendment Center?

JS: The First Amendment, those 45 words the founders gave us. Talk about eloquence! We are about raising the level of debate, dialogue, and discussion, thereby raising the appreciation and understanding for freedom of religion, speech, press, assembly, and redress. All of our programs are dedicated to raising that level of discussion with hopes that people will realize there is more to the First Amendment that touches their lives than they ever understood. Many people think of that amendment in a negative way, like an intrusive or abusive press or pornography. People are very cynical about the First Amendment.

PSD: This amendment is really the cornerstone of our country?

JS: Absolutely. It was actually the third amendment the Third Congress proposed. Polls show that people today would probably not ratify the Bill Of Rights or the First Amendment. Then you get into something like a Flag-Burning Amendment. The Supreme Court said that flag-burning is protected under the First Amendment, although when I see someone burning a flag it pisses me off.

PSD: But to remain a democracy, you still have to

protect the right to do that.

JS: You're right. If I had been born a Native-American, been screwed out of my land, been put on a reservation, denied an education, and the only way I can make any money is to work in a bingo parlor, I damned-well sure might want to burn one. If my skin had been black, and I had been treated in the horrendous way African- Americans have been treated, I might want to burn one. If I were a pacifist and wanted to protest my country's involvement in Vietnam, with the wanton bombing of cities where women and children were killed, I might want to burn a flag.

PSD: The foresight and genius of our founding fathers in creating the First Amendment astounds me.

JS: A legitimate question to ask is, "Why the hell did they do it?" The reason was that they didn't trust themselves with power. They had seen what the British had done with power. The founders basically said it was better to leave the power in the press to be wrong than for us to exercise the power to be wrong. I think it was the ultimate act of conscience and unselfishness to give up that power.

PSD: Are you distressed by the growth of the tabloid press and its constant focus on what seems to be the lowest common denominator?

JS: I have seen some of it that I deplore, but I have never seen any of it that I would censor. I have seen some I would censure, some I would criticize, but none I would censor.

PSD: Do you believe the media helps increase the levels of violence by what it programs, or is just a reflection of the culture?

JS: If you took every violent show off the air, I don't feel like you would decrease violence one bit. I just don't believe that. The larger question is whether the media should show some restraint in deference to people who believe differently about that than I do. And the answer to that question, in my opinion, is "Yes, they should." I think there is excessive violence and sex on television that is gratuitous. I don't think society needs it, and there may be some minimal hurt that accrues from it.

PSD: This form of media tends to trivialize the precious nature of life.

JS: There are a few people in society who may be triggered by something they see in the media. I have thought about this a great deal because it doesn't help my cause with the First Amendment. More self-restraint would be helpful.

PSD: Are you disturbed at all by these major corporations buying the networks and then controlling the news departments?

JS: We are headed in a direction now where, in a relatively short time, we will have five or six major media giants. We need to start worrying about that now. I think they will also be heavily regulated. So I am concerned about it.

PSD: How do you define success?

JS: That is a very tough question for me. I know that I would have to be described as a person who has been successful. The only goal I have ever had was to be a great journalist. My only ambition was to make whatever I was working on at the moment the best it could be. I have done the things I have in my life because they felt right in my stomach. There are reporters and editors I have touched and influenced all over the country. The Vice-President of the United States is a reporter I recruited. I see some success of my own in their success, and maybe that is vanity. But from my perspective, that is success. I am extremely proud of the fact that my son is a journalist.

PSD: What practices or principles have worked for you in pursuit of this goal?

JS: There are two things that I have always been able to do that have helped guide me. One is that I have been able, at times, to go somewhere for an hour or two and just think through problems. That has been a wonderful advantage for me. The second is that I have always had somebody around me who could privately come to me and say, "Bull."

Years ago, I decided you always had to have somebody to challenge your deepest-held convictions. I guess I am an intuition guy based on experience.

PSD: With all of your drive and passion in your vocation, was it hard to strike a balance as a family man?

JS: I'd say so. I'm willing to accept traditional definitions of success in terms of high achievement, but high achievers are not always successful. Remember, it is very difficult to be successful in every area of human existence. It is very tough to be successful in business and be successful as a father or community leader. I guess if one area was shortchanged in my life, maybe it was the community. I thought my position as editor precluded my involvement in the community. I was a member of the Rotary Club for a short period of time, until one day they refused to allow black members admittance. So I resigned that day.

PSD: Were you a difficult man to work for?

JS: The most important lesson I learned in my whole career was that power over subordinates is a monstrous weapon. If you are going to encourage subordinates towards high performance, you really have to be willing to understand how that power can punish. Then you have to understand that the people you have to work with on a daily basis have to be encouraged. They can't be intimidated and bullied.

PSD: What made you such a journalistic bloodhound?

JS: A lot of it is upbringing. I was raised a very devout Roman Catholic, and was brought up to believe strongly in right and wrong, good and evil, justice and injustice. I was lucky to be raised by parents who were very loving. I think I had a clear sense, pretty early on, of what it meant to be moral and ethical.

PSD: What brings you the most pleasure these days?

JS: I am really happiest when my wife and I are doing something together, particularly if my son and daughter-in-law are part of it. We have been married almost forty-two years. My wife was a professional pop singer who came here from Rome, Georgia. I met her when she was singing at a concert sponsored by The Tennessean at Centennial Park. She was singing there on Father's Day. I covered the event, and that's where I met her.

PSD: Legend has it you were quite smitten?

JS: I was, but she wasn't. (He laughs.) The first five years we were married she made five times more money than me. She sang with Arthur Godfrey and his band, and was very successful. She sacrificed a lot for my career, and after I became Editor, she rarely sang for money.

PSD: Do you thrive on competition?

JS: I am very competitive, and hate to lose. I played tennis every day for years and won a lot of club tournaments and trophies. I think competition is part of what has driven me all these years. The other thing was luck. My gene pool had some talent in it. My mother and father gave me some gifts that I was blessed to have.

PSD: You fought hard against institutionalized power blocking the rights of human beings.

JS: Yes, because that pisses me off. Like when they tried to turn the lights off at Fisk University because the school hadn't paid its gas bill. I fought like hell, and eventually we raised the money to get them back on.

PSD: Sadly, you lost your brother recently.

JS: I was the oldest, and the brother who was right after me — a bloody saint, a social worker — died last year. He was terrific. It was hard to lose him. Shortly after he got his Master's degree, he started a place called Richland Village, which was a home for children. I remember one night, shortly after becoming Editor, I was on my way home down some side street, when I came upon my brother walking along the gutter. I said, 'What the hell are you doing walking along this street?' He said, "A couple of the kids have run away from the home, and I was walking over to their house." I said, 'You are out of your skull. Go home, call the police, and have them bring them back. You go home and go to sleep.' He gave me quite a piece of his mind. I didn't understand that he had to be there for these kids. He loved those kids.

PSD: It sounds like he was successful in an entirely different way.

JS: I can talk about winning prizes and awards. But what makes a difference in life is a guy like this, who is a success, who gives of himself enough to make a difference in some kids' lives. All of us consider him the most successful amongst us. My achievements mean nothing compared to him. This man truly defines success.

PSD: John, are you a spiritual man?

JS: I was born a Roman Catholic and I am still one. That's not to say I am comfortable within the religious dogma of any religion.

PSD: How would you like to be remembered?

JS: I don't want to be phony about it, but I would like to be remembered. I would like to be known as a journalist who made a difference, but also as a father who made a difference. I would also like to be remembered as someone who made a small difference in the field of civil rights and worked in other ways to right civil wrongs. I relate to people who are in trouble.

PSD: Do you ever think of the miraculous wonder of being?

JS: Let me put it this way: My favorite poem is by Walt Whitman, and is in his book Leaves of Grass. It is called "Miracles." It says, "Who makes much of miracles? As for me I see of nothing else." Then he recites a litany of the miracles that are around him. I identify with miracles as Whitman, who was an agnostic, saw them. I have told my wife that whatever else happens at my funeral, I would like my favorite poem read. Whitman sees miracles everywhere — riding in a car, walking along the water, in the fishes in the sea. I relate to that poem in a very meaningful way.

MIRACLES

WHY! Who makes much of a miracle?

As to me, I know of nothing else but miracles,

Whether I walk the streets of Manhattan,

Or dart my sight over the roofs of houses toward the sky,

Or wade with naked feet along the beach, just in the edge of the water,

Or stand under trees in the woods,

Or talk by day with any one I love—or sleep in the bed at night with any one I love,

Or sit at table at dinner with my mother,

Or look at strangers opposite me riding in the car,

Or watch honey-bees busy around the hive, of a summer forenoon,

Or animals feeding in the fields,

Or birds—or the wonderfulness of insects in the air,

Or the wonderfulness of the sun-down—or of stars shining so quiet and bright,

Or the exquisite, delicate, thin curve of the new moon in spring;

Or whether I go among those I like best, and that like me best—mechanics, boatmen, farmers,

Or among the savants—or to the soiree—or to the opera,

Or stand along while looking at the movements of machinery,

Or behold children at their sports,

Or the admirable sight of the perfect old man, or the perfect old woman,

Or the sick in hospitals, or the dead carried to burial,

Or my own eyes and figure in the glass;

These, with the rest, one and all, are to me miracles,

The whole referring—yet each distinct, and in its place.

To me, every hour of the light and dark is a miracle,

Every cubic inch of space is a miracle,

Every square yard of the surface of the earth is spread with the same,

Every foot of the interior swarms with the same;

Every spear of grass—the frames, limbs, organs, of men and women, and all that concerns them,

All these to me are unspeakably perfect miracles.

To me the sea is a continual miracle;

The fishes that swim—the rocks—the motion of the waves—the ships, with men in them,

What stranger miracles are there?

~ Whitman, Walt. 1900. Leaves of Grass.

Peter Jenkins
(New 20th Anniversary Content)

Peter Jenkins is an American travel author. He is known for walking from New York to Oregon while writing two books that describe his experiences over the nearly six years that he spent walking.

Backstory: I met with Peter in a small restaurant outside of town and we shared a long, lingering lunch. We covered a lot of ground, but nothing close to what Peter has passed over. He was gracious, honest and very bright. We kept in touch after the interview, and the two of us even took a walk together.

PSD: Will you talk about your landmark book, *Walk Across America*?

PJ: Well, I sort of became an author by accident really. I was just a disgruntled young person from a wealthy suburb of Connecticut. I grew up in the 60's and graduated college in the early 70's, and like a lot of young people at the time, I just had a really negative attitude about the country and my future. So I decided that, instead of continuing to party like a lot of my friends were doing, I would try and do something constructive. I was tired of school so I decided I would go out and sort of have this boyhood-to-manhood life, which sadly our society doesn't really have anymore. So I decided I would walk across the whole United States and see if I could learn something about myself and my country. If I ended up finishing the walk and didn't like the country, I would just go on and find another country. Just like my forefathers did when they left wherever, Germany or Scotland or England or Ireland, to come over to the United States.

PSD: That walk created a book.

I got hooked up with National Geographic magazine because I was trained as an artist and one of my professors knew somebody there. I planned on taking 5 months and ended up taking 5 years and writing an article for Geographic. I was actually still on the walk when the first article came out. I was in Texas working at a Mexican restaurant as a busboy making $1.20 an hour, waiting on these blue-haired, Southern Baptist ladies. I would get all these calls from like the Williams Moore Agency and Hollywood and Robert Redford's agent—just people looking to see if I wanted to do a book. I ended up doing the book, which is called "Walk Across America," and it did real well. After the walk was finished I wrote the sequel to "Walk Across America" which is "Walk Less." I said to my editor, "Well, I guess I might as well get a job now." She said, "What do you mean, a job? You've already got a job." I said, "Doing what?" She said, "You're going to be a writer." And now I've written 7 books. So it was sort of a backdoor way of finding what it is that I could do to earn a living.

PSD: Big things often start from humble beginnings.

PJ: Yes, they do. One of the things that I've tended to do is write about my dreams. One of my dreams was to live on a piece of land of my own. I grew up in an apartment complex actually, and even though I lived in a wealthy community, my family was not wealthy. We were like one of the poor whites in the whole mix. So by growing up sort of rootless in an apartment building, I just always had this dream of owning my own farm and living on the land. So I wrote a book called *Close Friends*, which was a major adventure because when I moved to the farm I had no idea what to do. I mean, I knew which end was which on the cow but that was about it.

PSD: Are you farming?

PJ: Yes. I raise cattle and hay, do all the work myself, build fences, repair fences, pull calves. I mean, I've learned a lot. When I first moved there all the local farmers and native Tennesseans called me the "Bookman." There's the "Bookman," you know? "Look what he's doing now; he ain't got no idea what to do." You know, hauling hay by myself. I mean, I didn't even know what a gate was. I knew nothing. A lot of people think of farmers as stupid. But in order to be a farmer, you've got to be so good at so many different things. You have to know something about mechanics. And if you raise animals, you've got to know about that. You almost have to be like a veterinarian.

PSD: What qualities dwell within you that allows you to have a dream and then proactively pursue it?

PJ: One of the things that I write about in all of my books is fear. Because that's essentially the thing that stops people, the fear of failure and fear in general. We all are loaded with fear, even some of the people that appear incredibly confident are. All of us have tremendous insecurities and so on. The only way that you overcome these insecurities is either you let them defeat you or you sort of attack them. So I've just written about my fears because it's more like, if I could succeed, then anybody could.

PSD: Is the fear of what might have been always greater than the reality of the risk?

PJ: Normally. Although there's a lot to be afraid of. And you know, one of the things is that I tend to be pretty realistic and pretty critical about things. I've done some pretty dangerous things. "Walking Across America" was considered pretty dangerous. You know, by yourself just setting out across country with long hair and a beard and Yankee accent, walking through the South.

PSD: Yet we can take calculated risks.

PJ: One of the things I learned a long time ago is I ask for help. I do not, I don't let my pride get in the way at all. I've learned the lesson that you must subjugate yourself to people that have more wisdom than you about certain things because no one can know everything. In any of my trips I have always taken preparation very seriously.

PSD: You've been all over the world. Are people the same here in Spring Hill, Tennessee, as they are in China?

PJ: Well...

PSD: Cultural vagrancies aside...

PJ: Essentially people are pretty much the same. I mean, there's so many differences based on the system in which you are raised. So it sort of depends on what system you grow up in. That has a lot to do with the way you view life and view opportunities and the outcome of your life. I think it probably comes down pretty much the same. For instance, how a person deals with the roadblocks and the things that are thrown up in front of them because we all have that. I think we, in the United States, have a lot more opportunity. But a lot of people who grow up in this country don't realize that and don't seem to take full advantage of it.

PSD: Why?

PJ: They're a little too spoiled probably.

PSD: Soft?

PJ: Soft. People, in general I think, do not really want pain. And if they had a choice most people probably would prefer not to work really hard. If they had a choice they would prefer to be really comfortable, never cold, never sweaty, never too hot. Do you think you could ever be a great athlete with that kind of attitude? I don't. Because, in order to achieve, you've got to be disciplined and you've really got to push yourself.

PSD: But if you exist only in your comfort zone and you never push the envelope, you can never really know yourself on a deeper level.

PJ: Yes. It's an awfully boring life unless you really stretch yourself. You don't really have the opportunity to find out who you really are. So that's why I think there are a lot of people walking around on Prozac and self-medicating themselves in all kinds of various ways, whether it's through endless shopping or materialism or drug abuse, alcohol abuse, whatever. It's just because they never have the opportunity to really find out who they really are.

PSD: For the most part, did you feel welcome almost everywhere you went?

PJ: I did. And that was a huge surprise to me. I expected the "redneck Southern people" or "poor Blacks" to be the least welcoming, and they were the most welcoming. And then, ironically, the least welcoming were the people of my own generation—young hippies. They would drive by me and flash me a peace sign and keep going. I would be out there about to die of thirst.

PSD: I sense, in our culture, a quiet, almost underground movement back towards simplicity.

PJ: Well, in America we tend to never get enough. If you have a 3,000 square foot house you want a 5,000.

If you've got a 5,000, it would be nice to have 9,000. Although, like you said, a lot of people are going in the opposite direction now, I've noticed. I think they realize possessions can own you and a lot of people want their freedom and suddenly you have all these things. There's nothing wrong with materialism. I mean, it's great to be comfortable. I just think it's a matter of you controlling it as opposed to it controlling you.

PSD: What brings you the most pleasure these days?

PJ: Just walking around my farm; just getting out in the quiet and in a cold, crisp morning. Being out and the profound sort of balance of nature and watching life. I was just walking around today looking at the way my cattle were eating the hay I put out yesterday. Looking at how the calves were growing and how the cows were getting through the winter and then teasing my daughter. I enjoy an eclectic variety of things. I'm going to New York in a week, and I'll enjoy just being in all of that energy. The world has so much to offer.

PSD: Do you think we've lost something as a modern society because we're not in touch with the flow of the natural world?

PJ: Oh yes. I think we really are missing out in a radical way, and it surprises me that you'll have so many people that will not get outside but they'll watch "Discovery" all night long. I do think all humanity does have a really strong need for nature and not to be disconnected from it.

PSD: You spent an enormous amount of time just by yourself on your various adventures. Did you develop any kind of spiritual connection?

PJ: The best "thinking" and thought processes that I ever get into is when I'm moving. A lot of times when I'm writing I even get out and just go for a ride in my truck or in one of my vehicles or something. Or I just get on a tractor and it's meditative to me to just mow a field and go around and around in circles. I don't know what it is about the repetitiveness of a certain motion.

PSD: Walking does that for me, especially in nature.

PJ: Yes. Walking is the same for me, too. I've always liked to be alone.

PSD: You've been all over the world. Why did you choose to live in Tennessee?

PJ: The place I felt the most at home or wanted to raise my family was in the South. Then, when I started isolating the South as a destination, the place that I loved most of all, where I felt had this most wonderful sense of home and being rooted, was middle Tennessee. So I just decided to move here.

PSD: What would you say to your teenage daughter if she was about to go out in the world?

PJ: I would tell her to do what she feels compelled to do. If I felt like she was being unduly influenced by her peers or whatever to do the wrong thing, I would express that to her. But one of the things you learn about life is you can't force anybody to do something. So you let them make their own mistakes. When you love somebody you want them to be happy and support whatever makes them happy. I don't care if one of my sons wants to pave streets. If he loves it, go for it. I'll get out there and help him. I figure that's the gift God gave him.

PSD: Do you feel good about our country now?

PJ: I don't know. I alternate back and forth. I think our country has got some really, really serious problems. I think our politicians should be leaders. However, I think there's way too little leadership. These people are voted in to be our leaders and leadership requires difficult decisions. The Republicans and the Democrats and whoever are not really taking the kind of leadership positions they should and dealing with the difficult issues. I don't really think they will until the people rise up into some sort of a revolt and get their attention. Or doing stuff like electing Jesse Ventura, you know things like that. I love our country, but I think that we're moving in some pretty scary directions.

PSD: The people need to get more involved?

PJ: I think that's the key, and that's one of the main things that I said in my book "Along the Edge of America." I determined that, instead of complaining like I'm doing right now, what I need to do is go back to wherever I live and get involved.

PSD: Be pro-active and get involved rather than a complainer on the sidelines.

PJ: It's just way too easy to complain or be complacent, which is what I used to do. So I've gotten very involved in my own hometown. And we've got my neighbor to run for the Planning and Zoning Commission. Now it looks like he's going to be Mayor. We've got a lot of people to run for City Council and try to take a stand.

PSD: Peter, how do you define success?

PJ: I think the first thing to find out in your life, from either education or through experimentation, is what your gift is. Everybody has a gift. So I think if you can find your gift, whatever it happens to be, and then utilize it. If you utilize your gift, the world will be a better place. And then you'll be a happy person. I also think it's important to be a content and happy person, to be connected to your family and your community, to try to help others and help your family.

PSD: Don't look to be perfect.

PJ: One of the things that I've had to come to a place for my own life is don't beat myself up for the mistakes I might have made, which are plenty.

PSD: You think you'll always be a rambling man?

PJ: I think so. I mean the world is such a unique and rich place and I think that's my gift. One of my gifts is the ability to go to a place and bring it back, so to speak. I'm fortunate, because the vast majority of the people just can't all take off like I do.

PSD: People live vicariously through your work.

PJ: A lot of people would rather sit in their chair and have the adventure. It's like most of us wouldn't mind watching some of these movies about these detectives in the inner city. But most of us wouldn't want to really do it or have people shooting at us. I told somebody the other day that, if I ever live long enough to where I'm older and I can't move around as much, I'll probably have a wheelchair with 4-wheeler tires on it for just cruising, man. So much of what I do is just talk to people.

PSD: I always felt that after high school people should get in the world for a few years and really look around. Then, if they feel moved, attend college.

PJ: Right. I think so. I mean, that's what a lot of the European parents do. They encourage their kids to hit the road and travel. I don't think that many people know what they want to do right out of high school or know who they are. Sometimes you go to college and try to experiment and see what you're interested in, but still you don't have it.

PSD: Do you get a lot of mail from people who have read your book?

PJ: One of the things about my work is that when people read it they feel like they know me. It's like I'm their friend. And I get letters all the time from people of all ages. I mean I got a letter from some little girl, a 6th grade girl out in the suburb of Seattle the other day, and I got a letter from an older lady who just retired up in Pennsylvania—just all ages and emails galore from people, especially young people.

PSD: In a way you're giving people some hope.

PJ: I get a lot of letters from people saying that they're in college and they just feel like why should they go? They feel like robots. Like okay, you go from Kindergarten to 12th grade. Then you go through college. Then you go to a corporation and you work all these years. And then you retire and then you do this and then you collect your...like, why should I? And this guy was saying, why should I? I don't really want to do that. I want to do something different. But there aren't that many models for how to do it differently.

PSD: You're a beacon in a way.

PJ: In some ways people are using it as a model: If he can do it, I can do it.

PSD: I guess when you first set out on your very first few steps of your walk you never knew, you never really know, the impact single actions can have.

PJ: No, you don't know. You try to do the right thing. I mean, I constantly think about that phrase when I'm trying to make tough decisions in life around my family or around anybody. It's just to do the right thing. If you do the right thing then you're usually, it's going to come out all right.

PSD: Do you have any relationship to a higher power or whatever you want to call God?

PJ: Yes. I feel like I have. My roots are in Christianity and so I feel like I have a strong relationship with God. And a lot of the times, I really believe there is a God. Also, things that happened to me in my life, some of the things that happened to me that are so totally impossible, are messages that I get. I mean, even little things. Like I know if somebody is going to call me. Like they might not have called me for 6 months and I'll be typing on my computer or doing something, and all of a sudden I'll think of this person that I haven't thought of in 6 months and five minutes later they call me. I don't know how you explain some of that kind of stuff. I've just had a lot of things happen to me that made me think that there really is a higher power, a God. But on the other hand, some of my travels have brought me to the point where I have a real hard time being real exclusive about it, like condemning other people's because of their beliefs. To tell you the honest truth, this could be a controversial statement for Tennessee, but I don't feel compelled to turn everybody into a Christian.

PSD: Acceptance, respect, tolerance, are beautiful things.

PJ: Well, that may be beautiful to some people, but it's not beautiful to others.

PSD: Thank you though for being so honest.

PJ: Well, I've learned that honesty is the best policy. I was a phony Christian for a while.

PSD: Shouldn't we respect everybody in the way they choose to do worship?

PJ: That's the way I feel.

PSD: Wouldn't that be one of the most basic of all Christian tenets?

PJ: You would think so. You know, I hear a lot of people criticize some of these white, rural Christians for being prejudiced against blacks. Well, prejudice is just basically a fear thing.

PSD: Based in ignorance?

PJ: Yes. It's ignorance, but it's more of a fear. It's a fear-based ignorance. So I don't know. Some things are truly evil, like this guy out there in East Texas they dragged up behind his truck. And there's no remorse and I really believe that there could be people that are literally possessed by evil.

PSD: I think in all that time when it was technically just you, in reality you're not alone, in a way you're with something bigger.

PJ: That's the biggest thing, you realize. And that's really a great point. I mean, I think one of the major realizations was realizing I wasn't alone and that God was watching out for me.

PSD: Maybe there's so much noise in society and in our lives that sometimes to really get in touch with something higher, you've got to get out on a boat or you've got to get out in the woods to really connect with it.

PJ: Probably one of the biggest things in our society, more than materialism, more than anything, is busyness. There are people who are so busy that they never have the time and that's comforting to them in a way. Because, if they had to slow down and take a look at what was going on, they might not like what they saw, so they stay just busy.

PSD: Yet it's a short life.

PJ: Yes. But you don't realize it. You spend a lot of time 10 feet tall and bulletproof and that's when you make a lot of your mistakes. Normally when you're in that phase you think you're going to live forever and you're indestructible and your mind is indestructible. Then suddenly, in what feels like a few moments, you come to the end of your road.

Wynonna Judd

"Music has always been the outlet for my sensitive and tender heart."

Recording Artist

Backstory: I had sent Wynonna's office requests for an interview, but they always declined. Then fate intervened when she ended up sitting down next to me at the Bill Moyers event. After it was finished, we ended up talking for a couple of hours. It was an incredible conversation. As we were saying goodbye she spontaneously said, "Hey, I have no idea what you do." When I told her about the book I was writing, and that I needed just one more person to finish, she graciously said with a sly smile and arms open, "What about me?" The publicists told me I had 20 minutes tops to get what I needed, but once again we spoke for hours with most of it occurring after I had run out of tape. Wy was truly one in a million and such a sweet soul. I loved her. I was fortunate enough to spend some time with her here and there, usually the result of some chance encounter (We once spoke for over an hour when we ran into each other at a department store Christmas shopping.) Later, I met her mother who was exceptionally kind to me. Naomi and I once had a fabulous dinner, again by chance, where we spoke for hours about life and the mystery of the spiritual realm.

PSD: Your singing has a very spiritual quality. When did you first realize, "I can really sing. This is my gift?"

WJ: I knew you were going to ask me that question. This is sort of a two-part answer. I have always known that I was weird, that I wasn't like all the other kids. The second part of the answer would be that it wasn't until the last few years that I really knew, flying on my own, that my gift was such that it now astounds even me.

I feel very separate, almost like I'm two people. Because, when I step into the light to sing, I'm merely the vehicle of the anointing. Yet, when I'm outside of that light, I'm sort of like everybody else. I have told people before that I feel ordinary when I'm not singing, and that something extraordinary happens to me when I am. So it's an odd existence, because when I leave the studio, I'm just another goof waiting to make my next error, kind of like we all do throughout our day.

If I go through my day and start to feel arrogant, that doesn't work. I think that's why God put Mom with me for ten years. (She laughs.) Because God knew that I would have probably thought I was Elvis, and that I would be too busy with my head up my behind to pay attention to what the lesson here really is. And the lesson I have learned, in the last few years really, is just how truly ordinary I am, but how extraordinary it is when I open my mouth and God comes through me.

PSD: When did you first become aware of your purpose?

WJ: Right now, I'm thirty-two. So it's a very interesting phenomenon that I have only recently discovered. When I was younger, I took it all for granted. I thought I was bulletproof. I was too busy following after my mother, too busy reacting. Now I'm pro-active. I know the difference. So I spent the first several years of my success very scattered. To be honest with you, success is as equally devastating as failure, because it's not normal to win the lottery and the next day quit your job and change your lifestyle. That's a shock!

And that's what happened to me when I was eighteen. I was cast into a role of being traumatized by success and reacting to that role while just trying to keep up. Now I'm able to sit back and push the buttons, saying, "Yes, no, I'll get to that later." Balance has finally come into my life. So it's a very interesting journey.

PSD: Thank God you've discovered this at age thirty-two. Sadly, some people never get it.

WJ: Well, it's taken six years of Christian counseling to figure it out at $80 an hour!

(She laughs.)

PSD: You talked about feeling different, or in a sense, alienated. I know there are people who will read this and relate. That's a part of the burden of any gift.

WJ: It is a burden. It's a blessing and a curse. When I say these things, I don't want to sound arrogant. But when someone has a gift, when God chooses someone, I think it's because they have the heart for it. Even so, I have walked around most of my life with a "Why me, Lord?" syndrome. It's both unfortunate and fortunate that the reason I sing the way I do is because I feel things so deeply, maybe too deeply. For most of my life I've been "turned down." Yet, when I sing, I am "turned up." It's a funny thing.

People would say "Don't feel that way, Wynonna. You're too sensitive." But when I sing, people turn me up to eleven because they dig me. Yet when I am not singing, they turn me down, saying that I'm too dramatic.

I've always been this way, and it's really hard for me to be in a world that is so cruel and harsh at times. Music has always been the outlet for my sensitive and tender heart. I think that's why God knew I couldn't handle having a corporate job or being a mother with eight kids at once. This is what I am supposed to do because I have the heart for it and I'm ready to accept the responsibility and the burden of it.

PSD: What would you tell someone who's feeling a bit different and estranged?

WJ: The simplest and best advice I ever got came through a man named Don Potter. Don is both a spiritual mentor who helped lead my heart to the Lord at eighteen, and has made every record with me up until this one. Don said something to me that really put it into perspective, "You have to have the gift in order to do something." For instance, if you're blind, you're never going to be a race car driver. I meet people every day who ask for advice and I tell them, "If you don't have the heart for hearing and feeling the gift you have, then don't do it."

PSD: Whatever that gift may be?

WJ: Whatever it is. If you want to be rich and famous, be very careful. Much is given and much is expected. You must be really willing, and this is so important, because I hear many people say they want the authority but not the responsibility, and that is the ego. That is the part of us that says "I want to be the big IT!!"

I'm responsible for fifty people. And while that doesn't compare to a big corporation, it's still enough for me to go to bed some nights and feel a bit overwhelmed. So I ask people what their reasons are for wanting to be in the music business. If it's about going backstage to meet Reba or hang out with Garth, they might want to consider something else. Because it isn't about that. It's about an awful lot of really hard work.

PSD: Do you have any feelings about the times in

which we now live?

WJ: Unfortunately, I see a lot of people around me losing faith, and that is why I think your book is very timely. People are losing their way and are unable to hang on and have faith. They are missing the point that happiness can be found all along the way, not just at the end of the road. You must go with the process. For me, my music comes out of the need to celebrate and to praise. That's not where I was at eighteen, though. Back then, I wanted to be somebody and to be America's sweetheart. In the last five years, I've been slammed with a lot of scandal in the tabloids, things that have caused some really dark times. What I've learned is that it's a test.

PSD: Fame always struck me as a prison. It seems that a lot is projected onto people and what they may represent, rather than be about anything close to who they are.

WJ: This is true in some ways. I'm definitely the target of an awful lot of weirdness and I accept that responsibility. I sometimes look at Elvis and wonder what it was like for him to be so incredibly successful. Then I realize he's just like us! So, to me, we idolize and set people up on pedestals like they are such magical beings. I feel I'm being used through my music to open their hearts to God.

PSD: You seem to have a pretty good outlook on life.

WJ: Something I've learned is that 90% of life is really attitude. That's why you see a lot of people who may not seem very talented make it big and win the prize. That's why I try to wake up everyday with an attitude of, "What do I get to do?" rather than "What do I have to do?" There's a big difference. This is important because I'm of the belief that every thought you have manifests itself in your body. My mom does a whole thing on how important your thoughts are and how your body responds to those thoughts. She's living proof! It's a matter of your faith and your ability to believe. I keep one foot on the ground, one foot going forward, and my eyes to the heavens.

PSD: I have a feeling that you've become much more centered in the past couple of years. What effect has being a mother had?

WJ: God gave me a break. I have not had a great life when it comes to people being honest with me, even members of my own family. This is a very tricky subject, but it's important for me to talk about it for my own growth.

My whole life, I was always doing shows and leading what people thought was this incredible life. I had two families that never really got along, since my parents were divorced, and I was always in the middle of the chaos. I would watch people jockey for position with me because of my fame. And I don't blame my family any more for that, because fame is very alluring. It's just natural for people to be curious about people in the spotlight.

So I had to deal with a lot of people who have not been very honest with me. Now it has taken me thirty-two years to understand what unconditional love is, and that's when God sent my children, Elijah and Grace, to me. I think that Elijah and Grace chose me and this is the first time I have felt unconditional love. They are the closest thing to the angels. There is no purer love than what they give back to me.

PSD: What did it feel like to carry life inside you?

WJ: I sang the best I've ever sung when I was pregnant. When you're that full of life, you are obviously tapped into the heavens. Your feet are on the ground and you are getting fatter by the day, yet your mind is somewhere else. I daydreamed all the time. You're constantly aware of this being inside of you. You are absolutely caught up in this miracle.

PSD: How is the relationship with your mother these days?

WJ: We're closer than we've ever been. We finish each other's sentences. It's a very complicated dynamic. We are WAY close. It's almost like, "OK, Mom, cut the cord." (She laughs.) When I was in the delivery room giving birth, she was patting me on the head telling me I was still her baby. She's still my mama. I heard once that you are truly not an adult until your parents move on from this world.

PSD: Are you a "gut instinct" type of person? Do you follow your heart?

WJ: In my music I do, because I trust myself there. I lack belief in myself, though. But I have an incredible faith in God. I also know that, when it comes to my music, I don't have to worry. For some reason, I don't have as much faith in myself in my personal life. I have such doubt in my abilities. I'm just as desperate in my feelings at times as everybody else, and that happens just about every day. Once I tap into the outside world, I'm just a walking goober waiting to meet someone who's going to hurt my feelings. The only thing that keeps me going is my faith.

PSD: What brings you the most pleasure these days?

WJ: There's a feeling I have had — and I know every mother can relate to this — when I have just got Elijah to sleep. He's resting, it's peaceful, and all is right with the world. There is such contentment in the feeling that "my kids are OK." There was also a feeling the day after I had married Arch, a peace that surpasses all understanding. I had heard people talk about getting married, but there really is something different after you have married someone. There's this covenant. The third feeling would be right after I have come off stage and I go to my dressing room and take off my sweaty jacket. There's this feeling of satisfaction, "a job well done."

PSD: Do you do anything to stay grounded?

WJ: I'm a seeker, and am definitely on the path. I just don't have great discipline when it comes to me. I'm struggling to put myself on the list somewhere, but there are so many things going on, I sacrifice myself, which I know is wrong. I'm learning how to say "No," and take a few minutes for myself. I'm learning to replenish and rejuvenate. It's hard because I am such a doer. Five weeks after I had Grace, I was back on the road.

PSD: What do you do to relax?

WJ: I procrastinate! (She laughs.) I procrastinate very well.

PSD: I need to get you some of Anthony Robbins' tapes.

WJ: I met Anthony Robbins and he gave me all of his stuff, but I haven't got to it yet. (She laughs.) Mom laughs at me because she'll call to ask if I'm wasting time, and I'll say, "Yes." Usually, it's really late at night. I was up until 4:00 AM last night. My favorite thing to do is be at my house, put on my pajamas, put my hair in a ponytail, stay up late, and do whatever I want to do. It's the greatest! It's really quiet. No one is bugging me about anything, and I can drink straight from the milk carton if I want to. I'll do a lot of dreaming, and feel more like a human "being" rather than a human "doing."

PSD: Those can be such sweet moments to bask in...

WJ: I love it. There are also times out on the road in the bus that I can feel the same way. Like when the sun is just about to go down and it's really quiet. There's this feeling that this is how heaven will be.

PSD: How would you personally define success?

WJ: It sounds really corny, but our greatest journey is that to inner peace. I've been close to death a couple of times, once when I was delivering my daughter Grace. Inner peace comes from knowing that when I die, I am going to heaven, that I am eternal. That's a promise I don't have to question. Success is knowing that when I die I'm going to heaven, and if I never sing another note, I am worthy. It took me twelve years to feel that way. If I never make another record, I am OK.

PSD: That's beautiful. You are worthy by just being you.

WJ: We set conditional goals like, "If I lose ten pounds, then I'm fine." There's not enough celebration in life. I remember meeting Donald Trump and thinking, "You're really not satisfied with a billion dollars? Maybe if you get five or six billion, then what will it take?" For me, it's not about money. Now it's strictly "I am worthy; I am a child of God." Period. That's what it is for me.

PSD: What would you tell your daughter if she was eighteen and asking for advice before she went out into the world to find herself?

WJ: You know what my first thought was? "Go ask your father!" (She laughs.) That's such a tough question. I think it would have to come down to Scripture. There will come a point when Grace is going to know that I don't have it all figured out. I would tell her to trust God even if she didn't trust me. Take it to Him. I would tell her to follow her gut instinct, even if I told her something different.

Follow your gut. "People yell; God whispers." So I would give Grace this advice someday, "I don't care if it's a boy pressuring you, a teacher telling you something, I don't care what it is, follow your heart."

Your gut, gut, gut instinct. The instinct that is way beneath pride and ego, and the need to please others. This is the only thing that has served me through every situation. "People yell and God whispers." If I get still and quiet, I will hear my inner voice. So this would be my advice to her: Get still and know God, and know that inner voice. It will serve you the rest of your life, even after I'm not here.

PSD: Speaking of that, how would you like to be remembered?

WJ: I would just like to be remembered. "Oh, that Wynonna, she was a great singer. She sang from her heart." Just for someone to remember, to bring up the idea of me. To be remembered for kindness to strangers, for the acts of random kindness.

Patricia Neal
(New 20th Anniversary Content)

Patricia Neal was an American actress of stage and screen. She was best known for her film roles as World War II widow Helen Benson in *The Day the Earth Stood Still* (1951), wealthy matron Emily Eustace Failenson in *Breakfast at Tiffany's* (1961), and the worn-out housekeeper Alma Brown in *Hud* (1963), for which she won the Academy Award for Best Actress.

Backstory: I was blessed to know Patricia for years. But she would want me to call her Patsy. We met through her children during our summers in Martha's Vineyard. There was no one like her. She was an icon, yet she was also so real, raw and vulnerable. I spent hours in her kitchen over tea and coffee cake, discussing everything from her days in the film business to how life could appear to be so unfair and even whimsical. Her sense of humor was dry, her wit so sharp, and her heart was magnificent to catch a glimpse of in the right light. In a bittersweet twist of fate, I happened to be passing her home in Edgartown on the last day of her life and was blessed to share a last couple of hours 'catching up' as we had always done.

PSD: You grew up in Knoxville?

PN: Yes, I grew up in Knoxville and Atlanta.

PSD: How did you first get interested in acting?

PN: Well, I went to a church one Sunday night when a woman gave monologues. My God, I've never seen anything so thrilling in my life. My heart was pounding, my eyes filled with tears, and that's what I wanted to do was give monologues all my life.

PSD: Did you take to it right away?

PN: Oh, I loved it. Oh, I loved it. I loved it. Then I saw a play in Knoxville, Tennessee. Wow, did I have a crush on this boy who was in it. What a man! He was not a boy. I wanted to join, so I joined. I got in the play at once and it was so good and I was sensational. I got great notices.

PSD: What was it like to be famous?

PN: Well, I wasn't all that famous then or really ever.

PSD: Well, after *The Fountainhead*, you were certainly well known.

PN: Nah, not really. I wasn't. All right, maybe a little. But it's not even worth mentioning.

PSD: So fame is not all it's cranked up to be?

PN: No, not at all. Of course, when we had that accident with little Theo, that put everything in perspective.

PSD: Theo was your son.

PN: He was four months old at the time, and he was so sensational. I was at the A&P and I heard sirens and thought, 'What is it?' And I looked up and saw a police car whiz by and I thought, ' Oh God…' of course, not knowing my son was in the center of it. When I got to the corner, my nurse, our daily woman, she was looking for me and she said, "I hate to tell you but your son was hit by a taxi." And I said, "Oh my God!" I dropped it all and I ran upstairs. We went to the hospital and the doctor said that Theo would die.

PSD: Was this in New York?

PN: Yes, New York. A hospital way uptown, I think.

PSD: He was in a stroller and a cab hit him?

PN: Yes. Because the nurse pushed it in front and the taxi came and hit him.

PSD: Did he ever recover at all?

PN: He did to a large degree and he's divine. But he's brain damaged. But he's lovely, a beautiful man. About two years later my daughter, Olivia, contracted the measles and she died from it. She was only 7. She died of measles. (Takes a very long pause.) And that was... oh, I was just destroyed, really destroyed and yet I was strong in those days and somehow I kept us together. I kept everything going.

PSD: What does an experience like that do to a human being?

PN: Oh God, I'm not sure there are words for something like that really.

PSD: Do you ever get over something like that?

PN: Oh never, never, never. It's a very tough thing, and it's pure agony.

PSD: What was your philosophy as a parent raising children?

PN: I was a good mother, even though I had to work so often. I mean, I earned a lot of money in the old days.

PSD: You were the breadwinner.

PN: I was the breadwinner. When Theo was hurt, it was terrible for both of us. And then when Olivia died, I really...I was the only strong one. He just went to pieces. He really went to pieces. But I was strong, baby. And then when I had my stroke, from there on out. Othea she was just a baby when I had my stroke, and I was pregnant with Lucy.

PSD: You've had three strokes?

PN: Three strokes in one night!

PSD: How do you deal with such adversity and retain the wonderful zest for life that you obviously have?

PN: Well, you just have to. You just have to. There's nothing else you can do, unless you want to kill yourself or cry or live a miserable life, you know, you just have to go on.

PSD: To keep going…

PN: You've got to. You've got to, Paul. You can't be beat. You can't be beaten. It's tough to go on, but you've got to. It's a tough life.

PSD: It is, isn't it?

PN: It's just tough, baby. I don't know what's going to happen to me, and you don't know what's going to happen to any of them, but they've got to be strong. You've got to be strong. You can scream, you can yell. But you know, you've got to be strong. You just can't give up. I would tell everyone, you can never give up.

PSD: Do you have a spiritual life?

PN: Not really. All that, you know …I mean, there must be something when you think of it. When you see the skies, when you see this earth. I mean, it's just fabulous. Ah, it's summer and the trees are out. The flowers are out, and the ocean smells so good. Oh, it's all fabulous! So there has to be something. Just look at the heavens at night. There is so much wonder.

PSD: Life is so overwhelmingly miraculous.

PN: It truly is and I love it! I do not understand how this earth is so extraordinary and all other planets around us are just ice. Ice or fire or I don't know what. Also, I cannot believe in this huge thing that's surrounding it all, all this space. I simply cannot believe we're the only life.

PSD: Yes. I just was with Sir John Templeton and we were talking about science, God, and the possibility for life in other places of the universe.

PN: There must be life, all kinds of life, everywhere.

How can there not be?

PSD: Human arrogance would claim we're the only one.

PN: Well, we've yet to find it.

PSD: So we say it doesn't exist.

PN: How silly. No, think about this. It must exist. It must, must, must, exist. I sometimes wonder if they are aware of us, and what in heavens name they must think?

PSD: Do you believe in a permanence of the spirit and an eternity of the soul?

PN: I really don't know. I'm not sure we can know.

PSD: Is there something beyond your form or what we call Patricia, that is timeless in you?

PN: I doubt it. But you know, I mean, having lost all of my buddies and my father and my aunt and my everything, it's sad, but I somehow don't think you'll live again. I don't know.

PSD: Does the spirit live on?

PN: Oh, the spirit may. I would hope so and that makes some sort of sense.

PSD: In this state we can only assume. We cannot know.

PN: Absolutely. How can we? How can we really know? We're people. People don't know. But I'm very happy that I was born, even though, when I had my stroke, I wanted to die so badly for about a year or two years, three years.

PSD: That was hard, wasn't it?

PN: Yes. But now, of course, I'm so happy I didn't die because I adore what's on this earth and I will still travel and I love to. I love meeting new people or learning new things. Life is still full of wonderful surprises.

PSD: What brings you the most pleasure or fulfillment these days?

PN: I love to work. I love it.

PSD: How do you define success?

PN: I just think you have to know what you're doing, you have to work hard to get it, and I think you have to do what you can, the best you can. Then it may turn around one year and hit you on the chin or on the nose or something, but you know, you have to work at what you love all the time. I think it's terrible to laze around. I like to keep busy.

PSD: Do you have any fear of death?

PN: No, not one bit.

PSD: None?

PN: Not one bit. Not after everything I went through. I eventually came to a peace about it all.

PSD: How do you want people to remember you?

PN: Remember me with smiles and joy, for wonderful conversations like this one, for the laughs we shared, and even the tears.

Bonus Section
(New 20th Anniversary Content)

T.B. Boyd
President and CEO, The National Baptist Publishing Board

Dr. Boyd was open and accessible with an easy laugh. He took me on a tour of his publishing facility and regaled me with the storied history of the company. At one point we considered the idea of having the original copies of the book printed there in honor of his great-grandfather who was a freed slave and founder of the company. Unfortunately, we could not make the logistics work.

When I had the idea of donating copies of the book to seniors who were attending high schools in poor neighborhoods, T.B. immediately offered to cover the cost of the books as well as join me and speak to the kids. At one presentation we spoke to over a thousand kids and then stayed afterwards for two hours signing books and talking to the attendees.

Dr. Boyd and I also shared several long lunches and coffees where we would dive deeply into the challenges of society or the many ways one could achieve success. He was a gracious friend and mentor.

"You can work hard, but it is not always what clicks and jingles in your pocket that matters, but what clicks in your heart. While it is good to know all the dance steps, don't forget where the steps to the schoolhouse and church are."

Rosetta Davis
Graduate Student and Social Activist

Some people you meet for the first time and simply pick up the conversation wherever you left off in some other time and place. That was the case with Rosetta. When she invited me to visit the Edgehill Center I brought my guitar and sang for the kids. I became a frequent guest there and got to know several of the children. Rosetta was a selfless soul who was radically over-extended, both in the big picture and on a personal level. We ended up becoming friends and shared some lovely experiences together. I remember long lunches, talking philosophically on the trails of Radner Lake, and hot teas on cold days.

"Being able to make a difference, whether in one individual's life, with a whole family, or the neighborhood. If I can hear that inner voice say, 'A job well done,' then that, for me, is success."

Carl Carlson
Director, YMCA Y-CAP Youth Programs

When a dear friend told me what Carl was doing with struggling kids I thought he was a natural for the book. It took a while to convince him but eventually he relented and poured out his soul with raw, authentic truth. Walking out of his office I knew I had to support this man and his mission. So I hatched the idea of creating a scholarship program for the Y-Cap through a portion of the book sales. When I told Carl about this, he just laughed and said, "Well, I guess we will see." I could tell he didn't believe me.

With the help of the ever-gracious Ellen Lehman at the Nashville Community Fund we were able to set up the fund. In the meantime Carl and I would have lunch downtown at this greasy spoon he loved and share stories. Once the book came out I decided to just go ahead and donate all of the profits to the fund. One day over bites of deep-fried something, he confessed, "You know, Paul, when you first showed up I was frankly quite suspicious about who the hell you were, coming in and making these promises about funds and books, I thought who the fuck is this guy? Remember, I have heard so much bullshit in my life, I guess you could say my heart had grown cynical. But man, you were for real and you did it. Thank you." He then reached across the table and shook my hand.

Carl also gave me a great gift when he introduced me to the great Nelson Andrews, who became one of the great teachers in my life.

"There are many children in need around the world that I can't do anything about, but I can impact my little bit of society right here."

Phil Bredesen
Mayor of Nashville

As the original book was taking shape it felt like an obvious choice to include Mayor Bredesen, but would he agree to do it? At the time there was a big controversy on whether the city should fund an initiative to bring the Houston Oilers to town with the Mayor in the heart of the storm. I had also heard that Phil hated to do personal interviews. His gatekeeper was the fiercely protective, Tam Gordon. My repeated requests were politely turned down.

Then I had an idea, I wrote Phil a personal letter and sent it to his home with the basic pitch being: 'I have to believe you can spare fifteen-minutes to help some kids.' A few days later I got a call from Tam who said, "I'm not sure what you did, but you've got your interview."

I was given a sparse ten minutes but after a few awkward moments in the beginning I believe Phil realized I was trying to create something positive and he began opening up, even laughing. Tam sat there taking notes and nodding and things moved along nicely. We ended up running way beyond the allotted time. As we were parting I spontaneously said, "We should have lunch sometime." He agreed and said to call to set it up.

Phil and I had several lunches over the next decade, as Mayor, then citizen, then Governor, as friends.

"I think something that everyone has to go through is to finally recognize that the answers really are inside and that you ought to listen. You need to learn to listen to that voice."

Emmett Turner
Chief of Police, Metro Nashville

Chief Turner and I talked for a long time after the initial interview ended. We then had several lunches together. He was a wise and practical man who opened my eyes to the way things worked on the streets. Emmett also informed me about the personal politics of city government and his department. He was always honest and straight ahead with me. We even stayed friends after his retirement.

"I am always optimistic, because if I wasn't, I couldn't come to work. Some days are worse than others, but every time I come in here it's with a positive attitude. If you change one or two lives ... if you change a couple of things ... if you help people in this department... if you help people in the community ... then I feel good."

Betty Larsen
Yoga Instructor/Owner, Yoga Room

I took my very first yoga class with Betty, which opened up a whole new world for me. Yoga, meditation and mindfulness were the initial seeds of my awakening. Betty had a beautifully Zen approach to life and living that really struck a chord with me. Her energy was soft and open, with a rock solid strength as the foundation.

"I think if we all live long enough, we will eventually come to the understanding that God exists, that there is a supreme power, and that we are a part of God — the Divine power shines within each and every one of us."

Joel Solomon
President, The Joel Solomon Company

A couple of my friends suggested I speak with Joel for the book. At first he was reluctant, but after a few requests he gave me some time. I was surprised at the scope of his vision and his ability to see the big picture. He could be extremely matter of fact yet there was a spiritual thread woven throughout that found its home in the world of nature.

"Effortlessness is about becoming more and more at peace and relaxed amidst all the intensity that is around us all the time. I am choosing to activate as much as possible that is around me while staying at peace and relaxed. If I can do this, then I can become a channel for the values that I care about. And the main value for me is our planet Earth."

Jane Jones
Founder, Jane Jones Employment Services

Jane was the most easygoing person ever and her personality just filled up the room. She was a humble woman yet you could feel the force of her determination. Her laugh came easily and often. I was fortunate enough to get to know her after the interview too. We had lunch several times and she would always bring her elderly mother along to join us. It was such a hoot.

"The harder the challenge, the more I am inspired. I do not like the word 'no'. When someone tells me 'It cannot be done,' that really fires me up. There is always a way."

Joe Calloway
Motivational Speaker

Joe literally gave me the shirt off his back—well, the suit off his back. When I mentioned that I was considering getting into public speaking, he gifted me with two beautiful suits. He also gave me countless hours of his time in friendship. His wife, Annette Alexander, became like a sister to me. These are wonderful people who are extremely generous.

Joe is also inspiring, because he never stops learning and growing.

"I've become a real believer in doing what your gut tells you to. I say try it, go for it. You may fall flat on your face, but who cares? Don't be afraid of failure because, ultimately, you're not playing it safe at all. That's just guaranteed failure. Be bold!"

Jane Eskind
Political Activist/Philanthropist

Jane was such a loving and generous spirit who was always there for everyone. When we finished the interview she inquired if this was my full-time profession. After I let her know that I also played the piano professionally she laughed and said, "Oh, have I got a few parties for you to entertain!" Sure enough, true to her word, she got me booked into some wonderful jobs. Later, she even invited me to her home for a few events. If I ran into her around town we would always sit down and share a few moments catching up. She cared and wanted to know if everything was all right. If it wasn't she would want to get involved to make a difference. Politically, Jane was light years ahead of her time and a beacon for many to come later.

"There are all kinds of ways to succeed. One is to win the election. Another is to lose the election, but win the debate. Success is raising a family that's happy and well-adjusted and doesn't mind living in the same city as the parent. That's a great success and a great honor."

General William Moore, USAF (Ret.)
Chairman, Nashville Airport Authority

I expected the General to be an old-time military man like George C. Scott as Patton with tough- as-nails answers and a hard-shell exterior. Imagine my surprise when he turned out to be the polar opposite of my projected cliché. Bill, as he likes his friends to call him, was a soft-spoken, thoughtful man with an easy laugh and a warm smile. I fell in love with the guy and adopted him as a surrogate mentor-grandfather. We shared many lunches out at his office overlooking the vast expanse of runways and commuter planes. The two of us would talk for hours about an endless array of topics, nothing was taboo for the two of us to touch on. Eventually he retired and our contact became less frequent, his health slowly declined, and one fine day he passed. I felt fortunate, like many, that this man's kindness had touched my life so deeply.

"The first thing we need to do is have faith in the human being. The help you can give an unfortunate person to get on their own feet and take control of their lives is a hell of a lot more benefit to them than any amount of money you can give."

Carol Orsborn
Author

I met Carol at a cookout and we ended up huddling in a corner for an hour or so diving deeply into something compelling. Later, I watched her battle cancer and come out on the other side healthy and healed. She is always stretching and growing, taking off in new directions. She is wise and clever with a wonderful sense of humor.

"I believe that we have defined human potential wrongly. The western paradigm tends to think of human potential as the will and drive to achieve a goal. But it leaves out the potential to daydream, to love, to cry, and to feel compassion for others. That, to me, is the true human potential."

Henry Ponder, Ph.D
President, National Association for Equal Opportunity and Higher Education

A funny thing happened when I conducted my interview with Dr. Ponder. The plug the recorder was in was dead, so the entire compelling, soul-filled interview was lost. Henry was gracious but I was ready to jump out of the window. Luckily for me I was talked off-the-ledge by his kind assistant Angela Bevins. She promptly rescheduled us to talk and within a few minutes had me laughing about it. Not only did the second attempt go very well, but I ended up making the most amazing friend in Angela. In fact, we became like Soul Siblings. There was no one kinder or of greater heart. When Al Gore decided to teach a course at Fisk after his loss in the 2000 election, Angela got me a seat in his classroom. I used to take her and her mother, Ma Bevins to lunch or dinner and hear their stories of life and loss. Tragically, Angela fell sick and passed away far too soon, though I feel her spirit with me always. Ma and I have stayed in touch and she calls me her son. Who knew when I walked in that day to Dr. Ponder's office that I would walk out so deeply touched by grace.

"To care is the thing. To care about the plight of people who are in some difficulty, people suffering from AIDS, people who are starving in Africa. I would like to believe that any time a human being hurts, I hurt."

Ed Temple
Track and Field Coach, Tennessee State University and the U.S. Olympic Team

Ed was reluctant to see me at first but then he invited me over to his home and the interview was fantastic. He then spent hours showing me scrapbooks and sharing some wonderful antidotes. Ed loved 'his girls' as if they were his own. I went back to his home several times and he and his longtime wife were always warm and welcoming. He seemed surprised that I even had any interest in him, which always made me laugh. Obviously we came from such different places but we found common ground in our simple caring for others. His stories of racism and prejudice were heartbreaking to me but though they left scars, I can't say it dimmed his light.

"You have to be able to accept rejection because you are always going to have setbacks and you must have the will to persevere. Some people can't accept rejection, because they think it's the end of the line, but it doesn't have to be. You have to keep on pushing. This is what athletics instills in people — what you put in is what you pull out."

Dave Ramsey
Financial Consultant, Radio Host, Speaker, Author

When I first met Dave his show was only broadcast in the Nashville area and his fabulous book, Financial Peace, was self-published and sold out of his office or car. His passion was contagious, his joy obvious, and his life's mission a calling. I loved the guy and he was kind enough to let me drop by his radio studio, located in the office, any time and silently sit in on the show. We would talk at times about his dreams of expanding, but good heavens, did he ever exceed even his wildest dreams! Dave was confident, yet humble in his service to others. All these years later I sometimes wonder the vast scope of his wisdom and the millions he has touched and it truly is miraculous. I'm sure if I was to call him today and ask how he was doing Dave would simply say, "better than I deserve."

"What gives me hope and puts the light back into my eye is when you talk to a group of a thousand people and then come back a year later to find literally hundreds of them coming up and saying, 'There was something inside of us you touched. We paid off all of our debt and we are saving money.'"

Gayle Ray
Sheriff, Davidson County

About two weeks after the interview below, I called Gayle's office and invited her to lunch. She accepted and a beautiful friendship began. In the years to come there were countless walks, talks, some golfing, meals and fellowship. I watched and supported her run for Congress inspired by the way she constantly would challenge herself to go farther. Eventually I moved away and we talked rarely, but when we did connect, the closeness would immediately return. Gayle even came on my podcast and shared her experience in Washington D.C. at the Women's March. She is a special soul and I feel so grateful to call her my friend.

"I am a strong believer in developing the inner life and listening to what subconscious messages, or God, may be telling you in silent moments."

Reverend Carl Resener
Director, Nashville Union Rescue Mission

When I first moved to Nashville I had nowhere to go on Thanksgiving so I wandered down to the Rescue Mission to volunteer my services. I was shocked to see so many other people like me who had the same idea. At some point I ended up sharing a few moments with Carl so I asked him, "How many of these people giving their time will be here tomorrow or the next day?" He burst out laughing, "Today is the day everyone shows up. Tomorrow it will be just the people who who work here and those we serve." So I decided to come back the next day and many more after that. I grew close to several of the men who lived on the streets and though it was from my privileged perch, I got a glimpse into their world. Carl and I would have long, philosophical conversations covering so many areas, so when I decided to create this book, selecting him as one of the original forty-participants was a no-brainer.

"I've taken drunks, put them to bed, and watched over them. I've helped old men take showers because they were too feeble to help themselves. We've done unusual things to help these people. The impact comes from doing a lot of things that we don't have to do. They notice it, and this is sometimes a turning point."

Amy Kurland
Owner, The Bluebird Cafe

If you're involved in music and live in Nashville, you know about the legendary Bluebird Café. This is ground zero for writers and aspiring artists to come and share their gifts. Many were discovered here, but even more, many more never made it to the top. As a young songwriter I vividly remember my first experience there and coming away with the sobering thought, 'man have I got a long way to go!' The Bluebird is the extension of Amy and vice-versa. She is the den mother, the nurturer, and the gatekeeper. She is generous to the struggling and loyal to the famous. So it was an honor and a lot of fun, to sit down one afternoon in the café and conduct this interview. Amy was courageous and honest with her answers. Later, she helped promote the book by putting it on the website.

"Never be too proud to do the small stuff. I know how to run the dishwasher and bus the tables. In the beginning, you have to be willing to do any facet of what it takes."

Walter Knestrick
Builder and Contractor

I felt like Walter was almost two people: A super-successful businessman who was deeply connected to the power structures of Nashville, and an artist who appreciated the muse. Since he was also a trained engineer, he figured out a way to combine the two for the greater good. The more I dug around town, the more I found his fingerprints on programs that expanded the arts and helped kids. He was very low key about it and insisted I not make a big deal out of anything he had accomplished. At the time of the interview he was deeply involved in creating an art museum downtown in what once was the old post office. After the book came out, we became casual friends and I would go by and have lunch with him, brown bag sandwiches, at his office.

"I think if more people were involved in the arts and listening to their own souls, the world would be a better place to live. You'd find some relief from the rat race of work, providing for your family, and all the political things."

Muhammad Omar Ali
Street Merchant

I used to stop on 12th Avenue and buy fruit and enjoy these long, deep philosophical conversations with Muhammad. It took him a while to trust me and begin to open up about his own personal history. He invited me to come pray with him in the local Mosque, and I accepted. Prayer, meditation, and silence. To me it was all the same basic thing with a different name attached to it. I loved the Islamic practice of stopping five times a day to center yourself in the spirit and consciously connect to the creator. One day Muhammad informed me he was heading back to Detroit in search of opportunity because he was having a very hard time supporting his family. We kept in touch with a few phone calls and then one day I found out he had passed away. He went to sleep and never woke up. Just like that, he was gone.

"Once each of us recognizes that we need to try to do what is right, at that point we then begin to advance towards each other. You may be in India and I may be in Honolulu, but we are moving toward one another. Ultimately, we will all be gathered together in the end."

Susan Hill
Teacher of the Year, Tulip Grove Elementary School

My mother was a schoolteacher so I always had a soft spot for those who spend their lives in the service of educating our children. I know they don't do it for the money, glory or recognition since there is so little of that. Susan was a joy and of course we did the interview in her classroom after school surrounded by some of favorite pupils. Humble, funny and hardworking, she was one of those quiet heroes that changes the lives of so many people.

"I honestly care about each and every child that comes through that door. I want them to be healthy and to be safe. And to work at their potential. I care about every child here. So they know when they come here that I value them as a person and love them as a child.

Harry Bonnaire MD
Physician

I met Dr. Harry at a Christmas Party and the two of us spent a couple of hours talking in a corner. The connection was instant and deeply familiar. A week later we had dinner, then the following week lunch and our friendship was off to the races. He had come from nothing and was enormously successful but he did not forget his roots, opening a clinic in the poorest section of town. He also would quietly treat anyone without money who I sent his way for care. Harry had a huge heart and a passion for life that always made me feel like I should be 'making more of myself.' I loved the guy and when he I conceived this project he humbly could not believe I would include him among all of these notable people.

"You can basically look at human life as consisting of living, eating, working, and dying. But I think you need to transcend this, in terms of giving something back to the community, the world, and especially to the children."

Joe Rodgers
Venture Capitalist, Former Ambassador to France

I interviewed Joe at his office over a couple of boxed lunches. Though he was wildly successful and made millions of dollars, it didn't take me more than a few minutes to realize he still a country boy at heart. He was very forthcoming with his answers and easy to talk to about anything that came up. After we were finished he told me to drop by anytime, so I did. If he was free we would sit and talk about the town, sports, and human behavior. I watched him get weak from cancer, battle back, and finally succumb to the disease. At his funeral I was surprised when his daughter read portions of his interview with me from the podium. Finding after the service I was moved to tears when she informed me, "Daddy was always fond of your friendship and the book."

"It is nice to be able to do something that helps other people. Then you really feel good. Education is terribly important, but so is that desire. You don't have to make a lot of money to be successful. Just look at all the people who run YMCAs. My God, they are successful."

Ken Kanter
Rabbi, Congregation Micah

I met Ken's gregarious wife Wendy first and she introduced me later to her husband. I always though of rabbis as older, serious guys with long beards but when I showed up to interview Ken he blew up my preconceptions. He was modern, loved music, sports and more than anything, people. We talked for hours and he invited to come to the opening of the new temple. Later in our friendship, I got to hear him sing. Ken was really intelligent and stimulating to converse with on a wide range of topics. His door as was is heart was always wide open. That same big heart later took a bog blow when his beloved wife, Wendy died young of cancer.

"The whole issue of recognizing both the fragility and preciousness of life inspires me and keeps me going everyday."

Adolpho Birch, Jr.
Chief Justice of the Supreme Court, State of Tennessee

I had asked the Justice to be in the book a couple of times and he declined. Then Dr. Boyd invited me to one of their big dinner celebrations and I ended up sitting next to him. (Chief Turner was on my other side.) When the evening was finishing up, Justice Birch turned to me and said, "Call my office in the morning and we can set up this interview you wish to have." When the big day arrived I found Adolpho pretty fired up about a number of issues. He was combustible and fiery in the dialogue. Unfortunately at the time, I didn't have presence to realize it had nothing to do with me but his animus for the systemic prejudice this brilliant man had experience his whole life. To my surprise, he invited me back to visit and I went. I respected him immensely and he had a huge presence that filled the room. The Justice taught me a lot and some of it took me years to process, thankfully wisdom is a timeless commodity.

"To positively affect people is a good feeling, to realize that there are some people who may look at you and what you have done and what you stand for and say, 'There is a chance for me, too.'"

Patricia Reiter
Minister, Unity Center for Positive Living

For a couple of years I attended the Unity Church in Nashville where Patricia was the one of the ministers. We would spend some wonderful afternoons talking about spiritual matters and also the complications of personal relationships. She was wise, kind, and a rock to many people, yet vulnerable too. I supported when she decided to create her own fellowship. It was her who inadvertently began my speaking career when she called me post meditation and invited me to give the Sunday talk. Of course neither one of us had any idea what my topic would be, which was something we found quite humorous. The spontaneous speech that service was a huge hit and I went on to give several talks around the country on the strength of that opportunity. Eventually she left town and moved to Florida and I stopped attending any type of formal services.

"Inner knowing for me is a body feeling when you are in the moment of choice, listening to your spirit rather than your ego. You are weighing decisions back and forth, and there will be a moment of 'Ahhh.'"

Phil Hickey
Co-founder, The Cooker and Green Hills Grille restaurants

I met Phil while serving food at a charity event and we hit it off instantly. I later found out that the meals that were provided by his restaurant. When I told him that my piano playing jobs were a little sparse, he invited me to come work at his place for a couple of months before I departed for my seasonal job in Martha's Vineyard. My admiration grew for him with each encounter. After I moved on and he sold his place to take a big, national job based out of Atlanta we kept in touch. When I decided to do the book Phil was my first interview conducted in the Delta Sky Club while he was in between flights.

"I believe success begins with your purpose on earth. What are you all about? I think the real challenge is finding and having a purpose, a kind of higher purpose. I define success as footprints—not the numerical stuff, but the lives I've touched."

Dr. Bill Sherman
Pastor, Woodmont Baptist Church

Bill was the classic southern Baptist preacher, and though I have never been a fan of organized religion, I liked Bill and attended his church services a couple of times and was impressed by his passion for the scriptures. We met in his office and the interview was a joy with a lot of laughter. I went back several times just to spend some time with him and talk about life. He got quite scare when he battled cancer but his spirits remained positive. Bill was always open and generous with me. He loved God in his way and allowed me to love God in mine.

"To fight racism and to build bridges is kind of like shaving— you have to do it everyday. It is an ongoing proposition, a process, not an end result."

Thelma Kidd
Co-owner, Davis-Kidd Bookstores

I spent endless hours in Thelma's bookstore. It truly was my home away from home. The place was like the unofficial community center for me, and many others around town. The store also was always involved in positive contributions to the city. Thelma invited me to her lovely home for the interview and we shared a couple of hours in conversation. After that we became good friends who would meet for lunch or a walk around Radner Lake. I remember my sadness when she informed me that she and her partner were going to sell the store so they could explore other life paths. On the personal level, Thelma loved to take herself in new directions if only for the personal growth. Once they sold it, the place never quite the same feel and tragically ended up going out of business. It was a huge loss for Nashville and for me personally.

"There is this part of me that struggles between self-exploration and being self-indulgent. I don't want to be self-indulgent, but I do want to be self-respecting. To allow whatever is happening to happen, and to nurture whoever I am on the core level."

Duncan Callicott
Landscape Architect and Horticulturist

I met Duncan one day when I was visiting the home of Cal and Maggie Turner. He had such a wonderful sense of humor and sharp wit. For the life of him, he could not figure out why I would ever want to interview him for a book. Eventually he relented and we had a fabulous experience. I had lunch with him several times and also spent some time out at his home where I met his longtime wife.

"For what I do, you have to have a mix of creativity and love of nature. An appreciation of nature and a desire to enhance."

Acknowledgments

Thank you...

To all the amazing people who have read my books, *Hitchhiking With Larry David*, *Martha's Vineyard Miracles* & *Seven Crazy Days in Maui*, and let me know how much my words meant to you - through countless notes, long hugs, chance encounters, heartfelt stories and magical moments shared in presence.

I hope you will stay in touch.

To my oldest friends who also happen to be my amazing parents, I love you deeply.

Your life of sacrifice and service enabled me to embody a life of opportunity & infinite possibilities. You taught me that with enough hard work, any dream was within my grasp.

You showed me what matters most.

Lastly, your sixty-nine year love affair is a monument to caring and commitment. I feel blessed to not only be a witness to your story, but a living example of it.

Saint Eva... my spiritual sister and soul twin. Thank you for showing up and enriching the world with your love and light... You are a gift...

To a large group of Angels cleverly disguised as my beautiful friends. It has been such a privilege to be a part of your lives.

In no particular order...

To the Great Simmons and his lovely family. David, I appreciate your support and our ongoing conversations that always awaken me to a higher place.

James Weinberg for all the support and fellowship.

Brother Malcolm for the endless hours we share and grow together. Ma Bevins...! Montanez Wade Norm the Giver and his wonderful partner Jane...

Vineyard Family: Annie Pie, Mark & Ann Ide, Rita and Frank on Circuit, Bob Sparks, Sidney, Terrell & Kim, Priscilla and Ned, Cindy, Tony on 19th Street, Rabbi Jim, Wingman Kevin and the beautiful Ali & Tim, Pat and April, Vasska and Tarni, Suzanne, & Colin- thanks for taking care of my jeep!

To the wonderful people at the Edgartown Bookstore, who have created a magical oasis for all of us to bask. Way to go Joyce & Jeffrey!

David Sanford-my brother from another mother...

Jill McClure and her clan.

Conscious Community of Saint Augustine: Luci & Sam, LeAnn, Marian, Thomas, Kim, Cynthia, Brice, and Picasso!

Neil Warren, Robert Matsuda...

Matthew Wayne Selznick, who makes everything I do look and sound better. Thank you for creating such a lovely cover and the endless hours on my podcast. Bravo!

Peter Dergee! My dear friend, brother and producer extraordinaire, thank you for your unique and gifted perspective on my artistic undertakings.

To all the amazing people who continue to bare their souls on *What Matters Most* - I am honored to share a little space with you on this magical ride.

Please stay in touch!

Send me your Miracle stories

Email:
mvyhitchhiker@gmail.com

Please visit my site:
www.paulsamueldolman.com

Facebook:
www.facebook.com/paul.s.dolman

Twitter:
@psdhitchhiker

www.ingramcontent.com/pod-product-compliance
Lightning Source LLC
LaVergne TN
LVHW051823080426
835512LV00018B/2701